ALL FOR
WINE

Michael Modisett & Cindy Cheung

All For Wine / Michael Modisett and Cindy Cheung

Printed in the United States of America

First Printing, 2018

ISBN 978-1-7328402-0-1

www.2200inc.com

To Henry and James

Someday you'll understand

Table of Contents

Throughout the book we've added "sidebars" and "grapevines" to provide you added information.

Sidebars
Wherever you see this icon read on for additional detail on the topic at hand

Grapevines
Wherever you see this icon we're pointing you to activities elsewhere in the book that dive into more depth on a given topic

Introduction (How to Use This Book)

If you're like us, you find the prospect of reading a dense book about the history of Bordeaux or the terroir of Burgundy a bit daunting, especially without an actual glass of wine to pair with it. We've always found that drinking wine while simultaneously understanding what's in the glass is one of the best ways to remember what you learn. And learning even a little bit about wine can greatly increase its enjoyment. That's where we come in.

Think of this book as an interactive guide through the world of wine. We will walk you through 20 wine tasting activities of various skill levels. Our goal is to impart a bit of wisdom to help you figure out what wines you enjoy, why you enjoy them and hopefully find more wines you like in the future. You may even find yourself impressing your guests with nuggets of knowledge at your next cocktail party. Enjoying with friends is recommended! *Drinking while going through the activities is a must!*

In each of the activities that follow we start with a brief description and indicate which wines you'll need to buy. Don't worry, for the most part we'll be pointing you to a wide range of options that you are sure to find at any good wine shop and price point. We've included a pronunciation guide on page 95 to help you with your conversations with wine store staff. Unless stated otherwise, we recommend you seek out bottles in the $15-25 range that we find to be the sweet spot of price and quality. Spending at least $15 ensures you are getting a quality wine that's worth exploring, but in most instances spending more than $25 doesn't yield added returns unless you are an experienced drinker. While you don't need to tackle the activities in a specific order, we have organized them in a natural progression of difficulty and detail that you may find helpful. In the back of the book we've included an index of activities by number and type of bottle, so if you already know what you want to drink, use this to find an activity to match.

At a minimum we suggest you start with the first four activities before jumping into other activities that highlight individual topics. These first activities take you through the general elements to look for when enjoying any wine, whether it's the striking color, the deep aromas or the delightful tastes and textures of the wine. Subsequent activities will then expand on this baseline of knowledge. We've marked each as Beginner/Intermediate/Advanced, but once you've finished the first four activities you have all the knowledge you need to jump into any activity from there. Make sure you take frequent pauses as you go through the activities to sample the goods. Most are designed to last 45 minutes to an hour or more, depending on your level of discussion with your tasting group. Take your time, take notes if you'd like, and be sure to discuss along the way. Now is a great time to start a wine journal, and we've provided a template on page 93 that you can photocopy to get you started.

Wine is about perception, so there are no wrong answers when it comes to describing what you experience when smelling and tasting it. So be honest! If a wine smells like a barnyard to you (that's a technical term for wine that smells like manure), say it proudly! And candidly, poopy-smelling wines are some of our favorites.

Cheers!

Michael Modisett
&
Cindy Cheung

A Note on Temperature

Drinking wine at the proper temperature is crucial to its full enjoyment. Instead of getting bogged down in this throughout the book, here's a quick primer on the ideal serving temperatures for sparkling, white, red and dessert wines.

Sparkling

Sparkling wine should be served well-chilled, so get your bottles in the refrigerator at least three hours before you plan on serving. If you don't have that much time, you can chill a bottle in as little as 15 minutes by wringing out a wet paper towel and wrapping it around a bottle before placing it in the freezer. Once you've opened a bottle it's best to partially submerge it in a bowl of water and ice to keep it as cold as possible, or you can place it back in the refrigerator.

White

White wine should be served chilled, but not as cold as sparkling wine. A good rule of thumb is two hours in the fridge to chill, followed by ten minutes on the counter to reach the ideal serving temperature.

Red

Red wine should be served slightly-chilled, also known as cellar temperature. Note that this is several degrees cooler than *room* temperature. A good rule of thumb is ten minutes in the refrigerator to reach the ideal serving temperature.

Dessert

The variety of dessert wine makes it difficult to generalize, but typically the ideal serving temperature will be in between that of a white and a red wine, so roughly 15 minutes in the refrigerator before serving.

A First Wine Tasting

Level		Bottles		Price	
					$ $$$

Wines to Buy:	You have lots of options to get started with your first activity! We strongly recommend a red with a few years of age, but otherwise it's your choice. Ideally you'll find a bottle in your budget that's five or more years old as this will enhance some of the more unique characteristics we'll be exploring together. For a good value in an older vintage look to Spanish wines, especially Tempranillo [Temp-ra-NEE-yo], as they are often held by their producers for several years before being released to the public without high markups.
What to Expect:	Wine goes far beyond simply taste. In this first activity we'll walk through ways to engage each of your senses as you break down the individual elements present in a wine. And we'll make this easy to remember by outlining a simple four-step process you can use to enjoy any wine and that we'll expand upon in later activities. By the end, you will be able to better appreciate your wine's many nuances and articulate what you like and dislike about it.

There are many guidelines to tasting wine but there is only one rule: have fun! It's tempting to get caught up in analyzing every detail, but it's important not to over-analyze to the point that you aren't enjoying yourself. Many wines are just meant to be enjoyed without thinking too much about them, and there's nothing wrong with that. But if you've ever had a wine that tasted especially good and you couldn't pinpoint why, or if you want to better appreciate more complex wines you may want to try in the future, this activity is perfect for you. This is a great primer for the rest of the activities later in this book and may even inspire you to splurge on a special bottle you fear you wouldn't otherwise appreciate. Now pop open that bottle and pour!

"Tasting" a wine actually involves a lot more than just drinking. We know that's the fun part, but bear with us while we prepare you to get the most from the actual drinking part of the activity. Or if you just can't help yourself, go ahead and take a sip now, we won't tell.

Learn to toast in other languages!

Language	Toast	Pronunciation	Meaning
Chinese (Mandarin)	乾杯	Gan-bay	Empty glass
Czech	Na zdravi	Naz-drah-vi	Cheers
Danish	Skal	Skol	Cheers
Dutch	Proost	Prowst	Cheers
French	Santé	Sahn-tay	Health
German	Prost	Prohst	Cheers
Greek	γεια μας	Ya-mas	Health
Hebrew	L'Chaim	La-hi-em	To life
Irish	Sláinte	Slawn-che	Health
Italian	Salute	Sah-loo-tay	Health
Japanese	乾杯	Kham-pie	Empty glass
Portuguese	Saude	Saw-oh-de	Health
Spanish	Salud	Sah-lood	Health

Step 1: Look

Once everyone has a glass, hold the stem and tilt the glass away from you over a white surface so that the wine angles to form an oval shape like the image below. There are two things to look for here. First is the general color of the wine. Does it look pink, purple, red, orange? Good lighting helps, as does holding a sheet of white paper under the glass. The second thing to look for is the intensity of the wine. Try to read the text of this page through the wine in your glass. Can you read clearly or is it too dark?

The answers to both questions lend clues to the grapes used to make the wine you are drinking. Cabernet Sauvignon [Cab-er-NAY so-vin-yown], Syrah [Sir-AH] and Malbec [MAL-bek] grapes generally produce darker colored wine; whereas, wine made from Pinot Noir [PEE-no nwar], Gamay [Gam-MAY] and Merlot [Mer-LOW] tend to be lighter. If you already know the grapes used in your wine, you can use the transparency to gauge its relative intensity against other wines of the same grape. For example, if you are drinking a wine made from a dark grape such as Syrah, but you can clearly read text through the wine, then it's safe to say you are drinking a "lighter expression" of the grape. How much you like the wine would help determine your preference for lighter or darker Syrahs. See, you haven't even tasted the wine and you are learning more about it already!

The color and intensity of the wine can also give you clues about its age. Some grapes age more quickly than others, but in general wines start out darker and more purple and fade to become lighter and more red, orange or even brown over time. If you are using a bottle of Spanish red wine for this activity then it's very likely some blend of Tempranillo, a grape that can exhibit pronounced color changes over time. In its youth, a wine made from Tempranillo will appear deep ruby or violet in color. As it ages, such a wine will take on lighter hues of orange and brick red. Most red wines will undergo a similar transformation as they age, moving from darker to lighter in color over time. This visual transformation will also be echoed in the aromas and flavors of the wine as it ages, contributing to the unique enjoyment that can be found in drinking the same vintage of wine over the course of several years.

Step 2: Smell

Now that you've had a good look at the wine it's time to focus on its aromas. Bring the glass right up to your nose and really get in there – don't be shy! While being careful not to overload your sense with alcohol vapors, take a few short, quick sniffs to get an immediate sense of the wine's predominate aromas. Now hold the glass a few inches away from your face and take a deep breath, inhaling aromas of the wine along with plenty of oxygen as well.

What's the first thing that comes to mind? Do your best to keep this grounded and true to smells with which you are familiar.
Do you detect light fruits such as strawberries or cranberries?
Possibly darker fruits such as prunes or blackberries?

Moving beyond the fruits, can you smell oak, vanilla or chocolate?

If you are having a hard time picking out anything other than grapes at first, don't worry! Smells and tastes are subjective, and while there are common characteristics for certain types of wines, everyone is in tune to different aromas and flavors.

Swirling

You may have seen people swirling their wine glasses before and now is the perfect time to try it yourself! Swirling the glass introduces more oxygen into the wine which releases more subtle aromas. If you are worried about sloshing your wine all over the place, keep the base of the glass on the table while gripping the stem, and swirl. After swirling the wine do you notice any smells that you didn't before?

Perhaps there are floral notes such as violets or roses?

Or vegetal notes of green peppers or tomatoes?

Experiment with holding the glass at different distances from your nose and you may find that you detect different aromas from different distances, an indication of the complexity awaiting you in our next step.

Step 3: Taste

We know what you are thinking. Finally! Yes, finally, take a sip of your wine. Take two. Take another. Enjoy, you've earned it. Okay, you are through the boring parts now and finally you can get your buzz on. But before you finish your glass, let's reflect on the flavors you are enjoying.

Your tongue is capable of detecting thousands of different flavors, so to help narrow it down think about flavors in groups. For example, fruits, vegetables, flowers and spices. Based on the major flavors you taste, would you describe your wine as primarily fruity, vegetal, floral, spicy, or something else entirely? Don't worry about specific fruits or flowers for now, just general categories.

When it comes to tasting wine in a group, often people skip right to the drinking so they can make dramatic statements like "tastes like wet stone on a summer evening" or "this wine is the beach." Resist the temptation for such subjective descriptions and, most importantly, *be genuine*. Use descriptors that are familiar to you and likely to be familiar to others – we all taste things in our own way so there is no wrong answer. For example if you taste ketchup, say ketchup! If you smell baby powder, just say so! In future activities, you'll learn how some of these may translate into wine terms you'll feel more comfortable using around expert drinkers. Ketchup might be called "tomato leaf", for example, and baby powder might be an indication you are picking up floral aromas such as violets. For now just speak your mind and don't be shy.

Once you've identified your wine's major flavor groupings, pick one and try to be more specific. For example, if you are drinking a Tempranillo for this activity, common fruit flavors you may find include cherries and plums. Take a sip with these fruits in mind to see if you agree. If not, what fruit flavors do you taste? Grapes sure, but what else?

Light fruits like red cherries and strawberries?

Dark fruits like black cherries and plums?

If you taste vegetal flavors, are they spicy like green peppers or leafy like tomatoes?

If floral notes, is it more roses or violets?

If you detect spices, is it savory like black pepper or sweet like licorice and cloves?

What else jumps out at you?

There is no wrong answer, but there are typical attributes of every kind of wine based on the grape, region of production and age. Tempranillo commonly tastes of cherries, plums, leather, tobacco and vanilla. Have another sip to see if you can pick out any of these elements. Other wines have their own tell-tale characteristics, which we delve into in future activities. If you want to get a head start, check the table of contents to see if there is an activity in this book corresponding to the wine you are using in this first activity and see if you are picking up its major flavors.

Slurping

Finally, a note on slurping. Yes, it does actually serve a purpose! Slurping brings more oxygen in contact with the wine's surface which can enhance its flavors, as well as direct these flavors around your mouth and into your nasal passages so you can experience them more fully. That said, slurping will not make a wine taste *better*, it simply allows you to experience some of the subtler details that may be lurking beneath its dominant flavors. And do abide by common sense etiquette. Don't slurp when you are out to dinner or drinks. It's best kept to your private consumption or for wine tasting events. When in doubt, don't slurp!

Step 4: Listen

Next, while holding the glass level or keeping it on the table, tilt your head down and listen to the wine. Do you hear the ocean? Or perhaps passing traffic? Such sounds are indicators of...

Just kidding! (But try it sometime and see if you can fool your friends!)

Step 4: Conclusion

The most important question about any wine is simply, do you like it? Despite all the numerical scoring (such as Robert Parker's now nearly ubiquitous 100-point scale) for reviewing wine, a simple thumbs up or thumbs down from your own perspective is the most important critique. So what do you think of your first bottle enjoyed with the aid of this book?

Are you able to articulate why you did or did not like it?

What is your favorite part of the wine?

Is there anything you don't like about it?

Based on your newfound knowledge of how to describe the wine, what would you look for in your next bottle?

Keep this in mind next time you are shopping and see if your local wine merchant can direct you to something along these lines.

A Second Wine Tasting

Level		Bottles		Price	

Wines to Buy:	You can use any red wine for this activity. If you completed the **First Wine Tasting** activity, using the same wine will allow you to see how your judgment is already evolving after just two activities. Using a different wine will help you practice your technique in uncharted waters, unencumbered by expectations of what you should be finding based on past experience.
What to Expect:	If you've completed the **First Wine Tasting** activity, you already have a good idea of the basic approach to tasting. This activity adds further detail to the same four-step process followed before. The knowledge you gain here is essential when trying to find a bottle you'll enjoy from a store or restaurant.

Step 1: Look

You already know that the color of a wine can give clues to its varietal, age and intensity. Let's now further explore the wine's age by examining specific aspects of its color more closely. While tilting the glass away from you, examine the meniscus. This is where the edge of the wine meets the glass. Does the wine transition into a paler, more translucent color? This is typical of an older wine and in these wines, the meniscus will typically be broader. The wine may even appear as clear as water on the very edge. A younger wine on the other hand may have no discernible meniscus at all with its core color extending throughout the wine to the edge of the glass. Note the relative difference in the meniscus of each wine in the image below, with the wine on the left being the youngest, and the wine on the right being the oldest. It's hard to judge with just a single wine, but take a good look at the meniscus of the wine you are drinking now and compare to the next bottle you enjoy.

As an aside for white wines, a good trick to examine the color is to hold the glass at eye level and swirl to help intensify the color like the image to the right. This is especially helpful to determine the subtle shades of yellow in a white wine, and the results may surprise you. Who knew that New Zealand Sauvignon Blanc [SO-vin-yown BLAWNK] you've always enjoyed on a hot summer day is more green than yellow!

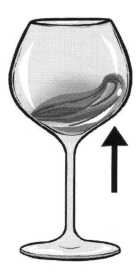

Step 2: Smell

Start by swirling your glass as you did before. Take a mental note of what you smell. Now let's take it to the next level to help you uncover subtler aromas in your wine. Hold one hand over the glass while you swirl it, trapping the aromas inside. The easiest way to do this is to keep the base of the glass on the table, and use the hand covering the glass to simultaneously hold and swirl it from above. After a few swirls lift your hand and quickly put your nose in the glass to smell again.

Are you now detecting anything you didn't before? Maybe deeper aromas of leather, earth or manure (yes, manure)? Not all wines have these smells, and they are more common in European wines than those found elsewhere, but look for these hidden smells lurking beneath the initial fruit aromas. That wines can take on such remarkable properties is one of the reasons they are so fun to drink. Look for even unlikely odors such as gasoline, a hallmark of high quality Rieslings [REE-slings], or roasted peanuts, sometimes found in certain aged red wines such as Côte-Rôties [Coat ro-TEE]. It's always exciting to find a recognizable smell in a wine, and often once you've uncovered it you won't be able to smell anything else!

One aroma you should *not* be finding is sugar for the simple fact that sugar is odorless. Thus wine (or anything else for that matter) cannot smell sweet. If you think you are smelling sugar, try to translate this into another more specific aroma. Common culprits are flavors typically combined with sugar such as fruit, cocoa or baking spices like cinnamon and cloves.

> The **Old World vs. New World** activity later in this book details the hallmark differences of major wines you've surely seen before. Check it out for a quick primer on why wine from countries with a king or queen are more likely to smell like manure and other fun facts!

Step 3: Taste

As before, start by considering your wine's major flavor groupings. Earlier we considered flavors of fruits, vegetables, flowers and spices. Are you detecting any of these flavors now? Take your time to find the major flavor categories and then delve deeper into specifics from there.

As you seek out subtler flavors, experiment with swishing the wine around your entire mouth which serves two purposes. First, this ensures the wine is reaching all of your taste buds. Second, this will slightly warm the wine and warm wine expresses more flavors. Consider the difference between gazpacho and tomato soup: the same basic food at different temperatures that highlight either the ingredients' fresh acidity or savory umami flavors.

Expanding further now, let's look for other flavor groupings beyond fruits, vegetables, flowers and spices. Are there any other major flavors you can identify in your wine?

Perhaps savory herbs such as rosemary or sage?
Or dried leaf flavors such as tea, straw or tobacco?

If you don't taste any of these, see if you can smell any of them first. A wine's flavors will often match its aromas which may be easier to detect. Earthy notes like mushrooms are common in European wines – with your next sip consider if your wine evokes thoughts of a damp forest floor of mushrooms and wet leaves.
Try to be as specific as you can with your flavor descriptors while keeping them relatable. Describing a wine as tasting like your grandmother's beef stew might mean a great deal to you, but no one else will know what you are talking about.
Many producers age their wine in barrels, so look for woody flavors such as oak and cedar or burnt flavors that stem from the treatment of the wood inside the barrels such as toast, smoke or coffee.
Finally, consider sweet flavors such as honey, caramel and molasses as well as flavors that we typically associate with sweets such as walnuts, hazelnuts, coconut or chocolate.

Are you gradually gaining a more complete appreciation of your wine over the course of a glass or two? Try to get even more specific with your flavor descriptions. For example, after a few sips you may identify a few major flavor categories such as fruit and earth. After a few more sips you may be able to get more specific and decide the wine is predominantly red fruits and damp earth. After a few more sips still you may decide the red fruits taste of strawberries and raspberries and the damp earth is actually more like mushrooms. And by the end of a glass you may be even more specific and realize that the strawberries and raspberries taste stewed like jam rather than fresh off the vine, and the mushrooms are soft and lingering rather than pungent and fleeting. So over the course of a glass you've gone from knowing nothing about a wine, to stating it tastes of stewed strawberries and raspberries with soft and lingering notes of mushrooms. Sounds delicious!

There's virtually no limit to what you can find in a wine! And your tasting experience will be even more fun with a bigger group. If someone finds a flavor that you didn't detect, see if you can find it with your next sip. Sometimes you won't, and that's okay, but sometimes when you do you won't know how you missed it before! And one of the joys of starting even a small wine collection is to taste the same wine years apart so you experience its evolution of flavors over time. That current vintage, bright red berry Willamette [Will-AM-it] Valley Pinot Noir may taste a lot more like mushrooms and herbs in a few years!

Step 4: Conclusion
You're now armed with a broader range of flavor descriptors including fruits, vegetables, flowers, spices, herbs, earth, wood and nuts. Based on this, what's your conclusion on the wine you are drinking?
What are your top three aroma and flavor characteristics?
Does everyone agree on this, or are different people finding different qualities?
In the prior activity you rated the wine with a simple thumbs up or thumbs down. Are you now able to be more specific, perhaps on a 10 point scale or a 5 star system?
If you think this wine thing is for you, now would be a great time to start keeping a journal of brief tasting notes so you can track wines you've enjoyed and those you didn't. Check out our wine journal template on page 93 to get started.

A Third Wine Tasting

Level		Bottles		Price	

Wines to Buy:	For this activity we recommend you use a familiar bottle you've enjoyed before, ideally from either the **First Wine Tasting** or **Second Wine Tasting** activities in this book.
What to Expect:	We're departing from our usual approach with this activity. Instead of stepping through our Look-Smell-Taste-Conclusion approach we're going to focus solely on specific aspects of your wine's taste. By the end of this activity you may find yourself the expert wine drinker amongst your friends. Or at the very least you'll know enough terminology to fake it!

In addition to enjoying your wine's flavors you are now ready to also consider its balance amongst three other components: sweetness, acidity and tannin. All winemakers strive to create balanced wine, meaning these three key components are in harmony, with no single element more predominant than the others. Each of these elements is desirable, but there can be too much of a good thing when out of balance with the other components. Wines that are too sweet, too acidic or too tannic can simply be unpleasant to drink. Go ahead and open your wine and pour everyone a glass. If you've had this wine before, as we recommend, quickly look and smell before you start tasting.

Sweetness
We all know what sweetness tastes like in food, but with wine the flavor is much more fleeting and typically only detectable on the attack, meaning the initial moment you first sip the wine on the tip of your tongue. After that the wine's other components, most notably its acidity, tend to take over. Most red wines are dry, meaning not sweet, but often "new world" style wines (from California, South America, Australia and others) in particular will have some minimal residual sugar that you can detect. If you are drinking a California Cabernet Sauvignon or an Australian Shiraz [Shir-RAWZ] for example, you likely taste some sweetness that pairs with the wine's other predominant flavors of blackberries, chocolate and vanilla. An "old world" style wine such as a French Cabernet Sauvignon or Spanish Tempranillo is less likely to have such flavor components and elements of sweetness.

Where would you place your wine on a scale from dry to sweet? Unless you are drinking a dessert wine it's almost certainly not sweet. Some non-dessert wines, more common with whites than reds, are off-dry, meaning somewhere in between. What does everyone think of the wine you are drinking now? Remember: when we use the term "sweet" here we mean sugar, not fruit or chocolate or other flavors we associate with sweets.

Sugar plays a crucial role in sparkling wines. Check out the **Sweetness Levels in Sparkling Wine** activity later in this book for a primer.

Check out the **All For Riesling** activity later in this book to dive into more details on the balance of sweetness and acidity in white wines.

Acidity

We aren't used to talking much about acid levels in our food, so this part may not come as naturally as identifying sweetness. One great way to find acidity is by paying attention to how much your mouth waters after you've swallowed a sip of wine. Much like sipping lemonade or grapefruit juice, high acid wines will cause your salivary glands to continue working for several seconds after you've swallowed. Low acid wines on the other hand will barely register and you may even feel your mouth drying out. An approachable way to classify acidity is in terms of apples. Consider if your wine were an apple, what kind of apple would it be: a green apple (high acidity), red apple (medium acidity) or golden apple (low acidity)? Based on this scale, where would you rank this wine's level of acidity?

Tannin

Where sweetness was mostly experienced on the wine's attack, and acidity was experienced on the wine's finish (more on this term in a moment), tannins are *felt* as much as they are tasted both while you are sipping the wine and the finish that follows. Tannins are what cause that drying sensation in your mouth from drinking certain red wines. With highly tannic wines you may even feel a sticky or dusty sensation on your teeth. Tannins are highly prized in full-bodied red wines so we'll have much more on this in the next activity, but for now simply consider if your wine has low, medium or high tannins based on how dry your mouth feels. Is it very dry and rough, almost gritty? If so it's fair to say your wine is high in tannins. Conversely, if your mouth doesn't dry out at all you'd say your wine is low in tannins. And of course if somewhere in between you'd judge this wine as having medium tannins. Note that despite tannins having a drying effect on your mouth, when discussing the "dryness" of a wine this has to do with its sweetness (or lack thereof), not its tannins.

Check out the **All For Cabernet Sauvignon & Merlot** activity later in the book for a deep dive on the role tannins play in red wine.

Let's pause here and reflect on your wine as a whole. You've enjoyed this wine in the past, and you were already familiar with its major flavor components before starting this activity. Now that you have a better understanding of its sweetness, acidity and tannins, do you like it any more or less?

If you like it more, why is that?

Is it a touch of sweetness that makes this an easy drinker, or bright acidity opening your salivary glands, or fine tannins contributing to a pleasing mouth feel?

If you like it less, is sweetness detracting from the more savory flavors, is a lack of acidity causing the wine to fall flatter than you remember, or are chunky tannins lacking a finesse to match the fine fruit?

With sweetness, acidity and tannins now discussed, let's move on to two other important characteristics of wine you are ready to evaluate: body and finish.

Body

Body is a difficult characteristic to pinpoint in a wine because it's essentially how the sum of all the components we've previously discussed come together to give an overall sense of the wine's weight or presence on a scale from light to heavy/full. A light-bodied red wine will typically be paler in color, express more red fruit than dark fruit, have lower alcohol and tannins and create a sense of direct freshness and liveliness. A full-bodied red wine will typically be darker in color, express more dark fruit than red fruit, have higher alcohol levels and tannins and create a sense of rounded weightiness and strength.

In trying to determine if a wine is light, medium or full-bodied, keep in mind that the majority of wines are produced to fall into the medium category. Consider it light or full only if it very clearly falls at one extreme end of the spectrum. Classic examples of typically light-bodied red wines include Pinot Noir and Gamay (aka Beaujolais [BO-JA-lay]) and classic examples of typically full-bodied red wines include Malbec, Cabernet Sauvignon and Syrah. Most other common red wines are thus medium-bodied. Where do you think your wine falls on this spectrum?

Finish

We'll let you insert your own joke here about how we've left this topic for last. This is an easy one. Consider how long your wine's flavor lasts in your mouth after you've swallowed on a scale from short to long. A short finish isn't always a bad thing, but a long finish is almost always a good thing, allowing you to enjoy the wine for seconds or even minutes after you've taken a sip. A long finish makes a wine especially appealing for food pairings as it's easier to enjoy the taste of your wine and food simultaneously. A long finish also gives you time to experience any quieter flavors that were previously masked by the prominent fruit and alcohol while the wine was on your tongue, think wispy notes of mint, smoke, licorice or subtle variations on the primary flavors you tasted earlier. There are no hard and fast rules here to measure finish, but would you say your wine has a long or a short finish? And do you like that?
If short, would you prefer a more "persistent", lingering finish?
If long, would you prefer a shorter, "cleaner" finish?

Conclusion

You've now added several new tools to your wine tasting arsenal. You understand the key components of sweetness, acidity and tannins that define a wine's balance. You can get a sense of the weight of the wine from light to full-bodied. And you can consider if the finish is short or long.

Using your new tools, what's your conclusion on the wine you are drinking? Does everyone agree the wine is balanced, or is there any element that stands out apart from the others? Most wines you drink will be balanced as unbalanced wines should not make it to market, so don't be quick to label a wine unbalanced. If any element does feel predominant, consider if perhaps this is the producer's intention and try to think of foods that might pair particularly well with this quality. Even a seemingly unbalanced wine may come into its own with the right food pairing. You can also assess your wine's body and finish and ultimately come to a conclusion on how much you like it.

In addition to giving it a thumbs up or down or rating it on a 5 or 10 point scale, can you now describe better what you like and don't like about this wine? Even if you don't fully enjoy the wine, with your newfound understanding of its many components is there anything you find interesting or compelling about it? Keep all of these points in mind the next time you are wine shopping, and feel confident in asking the clerk for a recommendation based on sweetness, acidity, tannin, body and finish.

A Fourth Wine Tasting

Level		Bottles		Price	
					$$$$

Wines to Buy:	You can use any red wine for this activity, but if you've been waiting for the right time, this is a perfect activity to splurge on a pricier bottle that may offer more complexity. If you completed the three prior activities, using the same wine will allow you to see how your judgment has further evolved. Using a different wine will help you practice your advanced technique in unfamiliar territory. Another option is to use a favorite wine you've previously enjoyed but couldn't pinpoint why.
What to Expect:	If you've completed the **Third Wine Tasting** activity, you already have a good idea of the intermediate approach to tasting including an understanding of balance, body and finish. Now learning how to systematically taste a wine will allow you to describe these and other details to others using common terminology, very handy when trying to find a bottle you'll enjoy from a store or restaurant. An additional benefit of understanding wines on this advanced level is that you will now be able to assess their quality, and who doesn't love being a critic, right?

Step 1: Look

There's really not much more to learn about looking at wine than you already know. One additional check you can perform after swirling the wine is to examine the legs, meaning the streaks of wine running down the inside of the glass. A fuller-bodied wine is sometimes said to have "long legs", meaning after a good swirl the wine will cling to the glass longer than a lighter-bodied wine with "short legs." Swirl your wine a bit and set it down to watch as the legs disappear down the inside of the glass. The legs don't indicate much about the quality or your expected enjoyment of the wine, but it's an interesting effect to observe.

Step 2: Smell

As your wine knowledge is improving and you begin to appreciate more expensive bottles you should now consider how you are holding your wine glass. This is somewhat a matter of personal preference that we won't try to dictate here, but it's generally considered best practice to hold the wine by the stem just below the bowl using your thumb and forefinger. This technique enables you to easily swirl the glass while avoiding unsightly fingerprints on the bowl. Some say this also prevents the warmth of your hands from heating the wine, though we've always doubted the slight warmth from your hands is enough to materially impact the temperature of the wine inside the glass.

If you haven't already been holding your glass this way all along, try it now and see if this makes it easier for you to control your swirling.

Enjoying the aroma of a complex wine can be incredibly rewarding, and you may find yourself wanting to savor it for several minutes before tasting. It's not uncommon for your sense of smell to diminish as you repeatedly smell the same scent. If you find your perception dulled after smelling a wine repeatedly, try smelling something else for a moment before returning to the wine. Coffee beans are a great aroma cleanser if you have them on hand, otherwise the back of your hand, a napkin or really anything can serve as a break. After a sniff or two, return to your wine and it will feel like you are smelling it again for the first time and you'll be able to pick out aromas you were "nose dead" to before.

Step 3: Taste
To this point we've focused on *what* you taste, let's now consider *how* you taste. If you've managed to avoid the temptation until now, have your first sip. Don't over think it, just enjoy. Now for your second sip, we are definitely going to overthink it.

Attack, mid-palate, finish
Consider your sip of wine in three distinct stages: the initial sensation as the wine hits your lips and tongue (called the "attack"), the remainder of the time the wine is in your mouth until you swallow (called the "mid-palate") and the lingering taste that remains after you've swallowed (called the "finish"). Leave it to wine drinkers to turn a simple sip of alcohol into a three step process! But breaking down tasting like this does serve a purpose. The wine's attack serves to prime your mouth for the flavors that will follow – an "aggressive" attack may prepare you well for an intense wine with bold flavors, whereas a "muted" attack may prime your mouth for a more subtle experience.

Sip your wine again and focus purely on the attack. Is it aggressive and biting, or soft and smooth? Remember, consider only the initial impression of the wine in your mouth, not anything that follows.

With your next sip focus on the mid-palate. Does it follow the attack, or is it a change of pace? Either way, what do you like or dislike about this? Do you find yourself preferring a harmonious balance from attack to mid-palate, or are you enjoying some conflict in the transition?

Finally, consider the finish. With your next sip pay attention to the flavor and the feeling that remain after you have swallowed the wine. This is where you are most likely to experience any lingering tannins. Do you like the mouth-drying feel that results, or do you prefer a cleaner finish? There's really no right answer – every wine has its own distinct profile.

Tannin
Let's remain on the topic of those tannins you feel on the wine's finish. Previously we've considered if your wine has high, medium or low tannin, and let's start by doing the same for the wine you are drinking now. As before, there is no easy way to measure tannins so this is somewhat subjective, but focus on how your mouth feels after you've had a sip of wine and decide if you'd rank this as high, medium or low tannin.

We're now going to consider an additional qualifier you can use to further assess the tannins in your wine. Let's start with an analogy: when considering tannins, think about the levels of sandpaper and if your wine's tannins are fine grit, large grit or something in between. Yes, we're talking about the size of something you can't see, but you can definitely feel the tannins in question. From here you can use any number of common descriptions for the tannins you are experiencing: chalky, rustic, round, silky, soft. The list is almost endless. But note that these words are describing a *feel*, not a *flavor*. Texture is the key to understanding and describing tannins.

Alcohol

One area we have not yet touched on is alcohol. By law, in the US every wine must publish its alcohol content on the label. Look for it on your wine bottle now, possibly appended with the suffix "abv" meaning "alcohol by volume." This is the amount of pure alcohol in your wine, and typically falls in the range of 12% to 16%, with some white wines falling lower than this and some red and dessert wines falling slightly above. For comparison, a typical bottle of vodka, gin or whiskey is around 40%. This is why you can easily enjoy half a bottle of wine but would regret doing the same for hard liquors!

Apart from looking at the label, you can sometimes estimate the alcohol level of a wine based on how it feels on your throat after swallowing. Higher alcohol wines may produce a lingering tingling or burning sensation. Have another sip and see if you can feel this. Note that well-balanced wines can have high levels of alcohol without you necessarily being able to detect it, as characteristics such as acidity and sweetness will affect how you perceive alcohol content. So just because you can't necessarily taste or feel that alcohol, it's surely there.

 In the US, stated alcohol level can be off by as much as 1.5% on wines labeled up to 14% alcohol. Once over 14% they can be off by as much as 1%. So that 15% Napa Cab you've always loved could actually be 16%. Be careful going for that third glass!

BLIC

With all of these techniques and tools to describe wine we want to share an acronym to help keep it all straight: BLIC. BLIC stands for *Balance* (the sweetness, acidity and tannin levels we introduced in your **Second Wine Tasting** activity), *Length* (referring to the persistence of the wine's finish), *Intensity* (the strength of the wine's flavors from muted to vibrant) and *Complexity* (the number of flavor groupings you detect in a wine including fruits, vegetables, flowers, spices, herbs, wood, toast, nuttiness, etc.) This is a great structure for taking you through the many components of a wine that you now understand.

Development potential

Whew, nearly there, we promise! You have just one last assessment to make about your wine before we come to the conclusion. This has to do with the wine's likely "development", meaning it's evolution over time. This is an area where only experience will allow you to improve, and even for expert tasters this is more art than science. The idea is that in recognizing how wines evolve over time, we can identify the ideal drinking "window" where wines are in their prime.

Most wines are sold in their prime and there is no need to age them further. But the world's finest wines, let's say anything costing more than $50 a bottle, will change significantly over time and can be categorized in three distinct periods: young, prime and tired. Young wines will taste overly aggressive with high acid, high tannins and an aggressive attack. Such wines will improve if properly stored for a few years at which point they will enter their prime. Wine in its prime tastes the way the producer intended: all elements in balance with clean flavors and a polished finish. But be careful about waiting too long. Wines don't stay in their prime forever, and if saved for too long will begin to diminish. Tired wines will have muted flavors, with acidic and tannic elements out of balance. A wine rendered undrinkable due to its age is considered dead. For an idea of what a tired wine tastes like, leave a half glass in your current bottle when done with this activity and taste it tomorrow. As much as you like it now, you'll hate it then. On second thought, instead of a half glass, maybe make it a quarter.

Step 4: Conclusion
You concluded your **First Wine Tasting** activity by giving your wine a simple thumbs up or thumbs down. You concluded your **Second Wine Tasting** and **Third Wine Tasting** activities by discussing what you did and did not like about it. With the abilities gained from this activity, you can now have your eye on applying your newfound skills and structure to tasting to a wide variety of wines going forward and ultimately be able to assess if a given wine is a good example of its type. In other words, does the wine express the ideal characteristics of its variety and region? A 10-year old Cabernet Sauvignon from the left bank of Bordeaux should adhere to a certain style and embody certain flavor characteristics that its fans seek out. A 2-year old Pinot Noir from the Willamette Valley may be equally as enjoyable, but should embody an entirely different flavor profile. A wine expert would know what each of these wines *should* taste like and assess its quality against this benchmark, rather than subjective qualities that differ for every individual.

You can also begin developing an understanding of when you should enjoy the wine in question: now if it's in its prime, later if you believe it will improve with time, or never if it's already dead. These four activities have given you all the skills you need to make these judgments. All you need now is practice and the experience you'll gain from the rest of the activities in this book. Enjoy!

A Boozy Movie Night

Level		Bottles	🍾 or 🍾	Price	Varies

Wines to Buy:	Depends on the movie you decide to watch. Specific guidelines below.
What to Expect:	Movie night is always a little more interesting when paired with a delicious bottle of wine. For this activity, choose from our list of classic wine movies, pick your pairing of choice, put your feet up and enjoy!

Movie: Bottle Shock
The Wine: Chateau Montelena Chardonnay [Shar-done-AY]
Rated PG-13

Founded in 1882, Chateau Montelena in the Napa Valley was at one point the seventh largest vineyard in the area. The vineyard stopped producing wine for a period and it wasn't until 1972 when the Barrett family (featured in the movie) took over and started production again. (Warning: SPOILERS!) Chateau Montelena's 1973 Chardonnay made history as the winner of the 1976 "Judgment of Paris", a competition that put the little-known and burgeoning wine region of Napa Valley on the international map.

The competition took top Chardonnays and Cabernet Sauvignons from both France and California and compared them head-to-head in a blind tasting, with nine prestigious and well-respected French judges presiding. Steven Spurrier, a British wine enthusiast (played by Alan Rickman) traveled to Napa Valley and sought out the very best Californian wines to pit against a line of highly-reputable French wines. Chateau Montelena competed with nine other wines (five California Chardonnays and four French white Burgundies made from the same grape variety) and took the top prize!

At around $50 a bottle, a Chateau Montelena Chardonnay might be a pricier bottle of wine than we might typically spend on a night in, but consider it a reasonably priced date night. Taking a sip of that delicious white is like drinking a bit of history. Bottles of the award winning 1973 Chardonnay and its red counterpart that won the same competition, the 1973 Stags Leap Cabernet Sauvignon, are displayed in the Smithsonian National Museum of American History.

Movie: Sideways
The Wine: Any Santa Barbara County Pinot Noir (includes Santa Ynez Valley and Santa Rita Hills)
Rated R

Set and shot on location in the Santa Ynez Valley in Santa Barbara County, California, the movie primarily showcases the Pinot Noirs of the area. The first grapes in Santa Barbara County were planted by missionaries in the late 18th century and, like most wine producing regions in the United States, ceased production during Prohibition. This region started to return to prominence in the 1960s.

Several different varietals flourish in this area, including Bordeaux [Boar-DOUGH] and Rhône [Rown] varietals and Syrahs as you move to warmer climates inland to the east, but you can't go wrong with a delicious Pinot. As Paul Giamatti quips about wine, Pinot Noir is "... *the most haunting and brilliant and subtle and thrilling and ancient on the planet.*" Note that Santa Barbara County is in Southern California, only a two-hour drive Northwest from LA, and yet its climate is perfect for Pinot Noir. This is because in that part of the state the mountains turn inland, running West to East instead of North to South. This geography allows the cool ocean air to reach further inland, creating a microclimate that cools the grapes in a region that would otherwise be far too hot to produce quality wine.

 Want to get a taste of the wine featured in the movie? Re-create Jack and Miles's experience and ask your local wine shop if they carry anything from the list below. Some of these vineyards offer online retail stores as well:

Sanford Winery – Founder Richard Sanford planted the region's first Pinot Noir and Chardonnay at this vineyard. Since sold and now thrives under the Terlato Wine Group.
Foxen Winery – Offers the gamut of wines produced in this region, from Chardonnay to Syrah and Cabernet Franc, and of course their flagship Pinot Noir.
Kalyra Winery – Taking influence from their Australian-born winemaker, this vineyard produces a full portfolio a wines including Australian Shiraz, old world Nebbiolos [Neb-ee-OH-lo] and Bordeaux style wines and a range of dessert wines.
Firestone Winery – One of the original wineries in Santa Barbara County established by the Firestone family of legendary tire fame.
Fess Parker Winery – Called Frass Canyon in the movie, founder Fess Parker is well known for his portrayal on TV as frontiersmen Davy Crockett and Daniel Boone in the 1950s and 1960s.

Movie: Somm
The Wine: anything will do. But for a laugh, go with a Riesling and have a new tennis ball handy. Why? Just trust us on this.
Not-rated

In this documentary you follow the journey as four sommeliers attempt to pass the Master Sommelier exam. It truly is "the hardest exam you've never heard of." While many organizations offer certifications to become a sommelier, The Court of Master Sommeliers was established in 1977 and holds internationally recognized standards. There are four levels of certification, with the Master Sommelier Diploma Exam being the highest. Fewer than 250 people worldwide have passed the Master Sommelier exam since the Master Sommelier Diploma was introduced in 1969. While watching this movie, ask yourself if the people on the screen seem to be enjoying themselves at any point of their preparation. What motivates them? Would going through this process make you like wine more or less?

Movie: Mondovino
The Wine: Any wine produced by Robert Mondavi (his name in big bold letters on any of his bottlings will make them obvious) or a wine from any of the innumerable, small producers throughout the old world (ask your local wine merchant for a recommendation and be sure to get a bit about the history or process behind the label since this is what the movie is all about.)
Rated PG-13

Another documentary with such a broad and ambitious scope that you may feel it drags in the last hour. But everything leading up to that is a great example of the battle between traditional wine producers and their more modern competitors. Think of this as David vs. Goliath, local vs. global, vine-first vs. marketing-first, art vs. science, family-owned vs. publicly-traded, resistors vs. collaborators, farmers vs. businessmen.

You'll get the idea pretty quickly as the film jumps from Aimé Guibert quietly strolling the gentle hills of Languedoc to Michelle Rolland cackling in the back of his chauffeur-driven Mercedes in various locales throughout the world. Several incredible wines would pair well with this film's wine tour of the world including Chateau Mouton or Opus One. But as these bottles can set you back several hundred dollars each, in their place we'd recommend any wine by Robert Mondavi (easy to find at just about any wine merchant) and a bottle from any small producer in the Languedoc region of France (Daumas Gassac is featured in the movie but may be hard to find so just ask your local knowledgeable wine merchant for a recommendation).

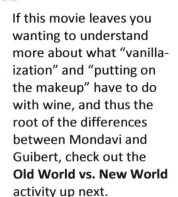 If this movie leaves you wanting to understand more about what "vanilla-ization" and "putting on the makeup" have to do with wine, and thus the root of the differences between Mondavi and Guibert, check out the **Old World vs. New World** activity up next.

 The repeated examples of Michel Rolland's advice to his various clients to "micro-oxygenate" may be a bit unfair to the master wine consultant, but it does make an important point. The micro-oxygenation process aims to mimic the effects of traditional barrel maturation with greater control and in a shorter period of time by introducing small amounts of oxygen to a large chamber of young wine. This can be done at various stages of the wine-making process and in various doses, thus in the movie you see Rolland visiting wine producers over time and providing his recommendations based on what he is tasting in the young wine at that moment in the fermentation or maturation periods. This technique became popular starting in Bordeaux in the late 1990s and is now used by winemakers around the world as it helps produce wine that is more approachable in its youth and therefore more likely to receive high scores from professional tasters and command a higher market price earlier in the wine's life. As a relatively new technique in winemaking, it is far less popular with traditional wine producers, and so you can see the contrast shown in the film between Rolland as a modern winemaker and Guibert as a traditionalist. The filmmaker shows Rolland telling all of his clients to micro-oxygenate, giving the viewer the impression that his advice to all clients is the same. This ties in with one of the major themes of the movie contrasting traditional and individualist producers creating unique wines versus the mass-market producers creating generic wines for wider consumption. Admittedly though, we think some of those "generic wines" can be quite delicious.

Bonus Movie: Barolo Boys
The Wine: Any Barolo will do, bonus points if you can find anything by Elio Altare
Rated G

This 1-hour documentary did not receive a wide release but can be purchased from the website www.baroloboysthemovie.com. The film offers an intimate view of the struggle between generations of wine producers in one of the world's most famous wine regions. A must-watch for any lover of Nebbiolo. We'll avoid spoilers and simply leave it at that.

Old World vs. New World

Level		Bottles		Price	

Wines to Buy:	For this activity we recommend two bottles of red since they will more prominently display the differences between old and new world styles. You have many options, but it's important that both bottles are made from the same grape (for example, two Merlots or two Cabernet Sauvignons), are of roughly the same vintage (no more than a year apart) and of course come from different parts of the world (one old world and one new world). A few options that would work well include a Pinot Noir from Burgundy France and another from New Zealand, a Merlot or Cabernet Sauvignon from Bordeaux France and another from the West Coast of the United States or a Malbec from Cahors (Kay-HOR), France and another from Chile or Argentina.
What to Expect:	"How do you distinguish old world from new world? If it had a king or queen in the 1500s (eg: France, Italy, Spain) it is old world; and any place they sent explorers (eg: United States) or prisoners (eg: Australia) is new world."
	- Greg Harrington, Master Sommelier
	Well, actually it's a little more complicated than that as the terms "old world" and "new world" increasingly refer to the style of wine rather than simply its country of origin. Learn what it means to drink an old world vs. new world style of wine and understand why this distinction evolved over time as you discover your own preferences.

Old World

New World

Go ahead and open both of your bottles and pour everyone a glass of each. You'll want to be able to smell and taste the wines side by side rather than one after another.

Old World Countries & Styles

Most of today's major wine-producing regions in Europe were established during the Roman Imperial Era roughly spanning the 1st through 4th centuries AD. Over the many years since, while each region in Europe developed its own techniques specialized to the regional grapes that grew best, they shared many common characteristics that persist to this day. Wine growers were often farmers and felt a strong connection to the earth. They generally tended to their vines with minimal intrusion, letting nature play the driving role in developing the grapes and thus determining the flavor of the resulting wine. This "hands off" approach continues to this day, with many European wine growers adhering to traditional methods of grape selection, vine pruning and spacing, harvest timing and disease treatment in the vineyard.

In old world wines, *where* the grapes are grown is more important than the name of the producer. Furthermore, most wine producing regions in the old world have strict rules and regulations governing the grape varieties that can be grown in that area. For these reasons most old world wines are named after the place they are from. For example, a wine made from the Pinot Noir grape in the Burgundy region of France will be called a "Burgundy". This naming convention allows the consumer to better understand the type of wine they are drinking since they can draw on additional knowledge of the Burgundy wine-making tradition and resulting style.

A major driving characteristic of old world wines is entwined with the culture – wine was considered to be best experienced with a meal, and so should be made in a way that complements, rather than overwhelms, the food. Predominant flavors of wines produced in the old world style include earth, vegetal, spice, and even barnyard. These wines also tend to be leaner with higher tannins and acidity.

Start by smelling the glass of old world wine in front of you. To help heighten the aromas you may wish to swirl the glass which will bring more oxygen in contact with the wine and "open it up." Do you detect any aromas of dirt or manure? Though you wouldn't think so at first, these are two highly sought-after aromas in old world style wines.

Take a sip and consider what else you notice. Vegetables such as green peppers or jalapenos perhaps? Maybe spices such as black pepper or cloves? These are all tell-tale aromas and flavors of old world style wines!

New World Countries & Styles

As the world was colonized and grapes began to be grown in more distant locations, producers no longer felt tied to the traditions of their home regions. They experienced a freedom to experiment with new techniques that would have been considered blasphemous in their native lands, and a willingness to introduce new grape varieties to their regions. They also showed a willingness to play a driving role in shaping the flavor of the wine by lengthening hang time on the vine, treating for disease, adding nutrients to the soil and bringing more advanced scientific techniques such as "cryo-extraction" and "thermo-vinification" into the fermenting process.

Most new world wines are named after the predominate grape. For example, a wine made from the Pinot Noir grape in the Willamette Valley of Oregon will be called a Pinot Noir rather than a "Willamette."

Compared to the old world convention of naming the wine for its place or origin, this approach is more immediately transparent about its grape variety, but less-forthcoming about locale.

Contrasted with the culture of the old world countries, people in the new world were happy to drink wine on its own without the accompaniment of food. As a result, wines could be made stronger, sweeter and more alcoholic without fear of over-powering a meal. Predominant flavors of wines produced in the new world style include fruit, floral and vanilla. These wines tend to be softer, richer, sweeter and more boldly flavored with oak.

So now smell and taste your glass of new world wine. Do you detect a sweeter profile, possibly with notes of chocolate, vanilla and very ripe dark fruit? These are all typical attributes of a new world style wine.

Your verdict

Now that you've experienced a little of each wine, smell them both next to each other. How do they compare? If you close your eyes and have someone else move the glasses around, are you able to detect which is which based purely on the smell? You might find the new world wine is more "fruity", where the old world wine is more "funky."

While keeping your eyes closed, now have someone hand you one of the two wines and try the same process while tasting the wine. Does that make the contrast even more clear?

In addition to the differences you are starting to identify, do you find that they share characteristics as well? Being made from the same grape and of similar age means they could potentially share many characteristics behind the expressions of each producer.

So do you have a preference? Are you enjoying the more natural earthy flavors of the old world wine? Or do you prefer the sweeter, fruitier taste of the new world?

For many people in the US, old world style wines are an acquired taste. This is no surprise since, after all, who likes to eat dirt and manure? And for this reason most US grocery store wines in the $10 range are going to be in the new world style. But give your palate time to develop, and think of what types of food you might enjoy with your preferred wine. And the next time you are out to dinner and looking for a recommendation you can give your sommelier some guidance on your preferred style.

Classic Wine Pairings: When 1 + 1 = 3

Level		Bottles		Price	Varies

Wines to Buy:	You have so many options for this activity we recommend first skimming through to see what piques your interest, narrowing it down to one or two food/wine pairings and concentrating on those. You can revisit this activity to try out each combination and later look to identify your own. The possibilities are endless and this activity will give you some general guidelines to help direct your own discovery process.
What to Expect:	Wine is such an important part of a complete dining experience. We will try a few classic wine and food pairings that illustrate basic guidelines for discovering new pairings on your own. Of all the activities in this book, this is the one that most benefits from your own experimentation, so after covering the basics be sure to venture out to uncover your own personal favorite pairing!

Why wine pairs so well with food

Wine snobs might say that wine can stand on its own, appreciated without other sensory influences that distract from its enjoyment in the pure, but that good food, on the other hand, demands wine that will accentuate the food's nuances and enrich enjoyment of its flavors and aromas. While there are many wines that taste great on their own, historically wine was meant to be just one component of a meal, and that's the focus of this activity. Our belief is that nearly all wine is improved when enjoyed with food and vice versa.

The descriptions on the back label of some bottles of wine will often steer you in a certain direction. It's common, for instance, to read on a California Chardonnay a generic description like "pair with rich cheeses, fish and poultry." Similarly, many high-end restaurants offer suggested wine pairings with their menu. Typical examples include sparkling wines with appetizers, white wines with fish, red wines with meat and sweet wines with dessert. These menu pairings are illustrative of the one general principle of matching wine to food: at its most basic, try to match the weight of the wine with the food.

Lighter foods (such as the salads, vegetables and shell fish often comprising appetizers) pair well with lighter wines such as delicate whites including Sauvignon Blanc and Pinot Grigio [PEE-no GREE-jee-oh] or anything sparkling such as Champagne [SHAM-pain], Cava [KAH-va] and Prosecco [Pro-SEK-oh].

As the menu progresses into first courses, the weight and richness of the dishes will gradually intensify into heartier food such as pasta, fish and white meat that demand a more robust wine. In these cases you may find fuller-bodied white wines such as oaked Chardonnay or lighter red wines such as Pinot Noir and Gamay more appropriate to match the weight of the dishes.

Next, the menu will move into second or main courses, often consisting of red meat and game. Here a heavy, full-bodied wine is required. Powerful red wines such as Cabernet Sauvignon and Syrah will be the standard recommendations to hold up to the strength of the food.

Finally with dessert a common suggestion is to enjoy a wine with enough sweetness to match the food including a huge class of dessert wines from around the world. And further still, appropriate dessert pairings extend far beyond the reach of this book and include such lofty spirits as cognac (still grape based!), whiskey (Bourbon, Scotch and others) and innumerable other digestives (a catch-all term encompassing anything designed for optimal enjoyment following a meal).

For now, the thought process behind these pairings is more important that the specific recommendations. A good pairing will match food and wine of similar weights, with enough in common to avoid clashing, but enough in contrast to bring out the fullest, deepest, brightest flavors of each. This nuanced balance of similarities and differences between the food and wine is what makes finding a perfect pairing so difficult, and so fun!

Classic wine pairings to try
Several combinations of food and wine have been so consistently enjoyed throughout history that they are considered the standards for classic pairings. These serve as examples of why certain flavor combinations produce a result greater than the sum of their individual components. Here are a few examples of classic pairings, along with a description of why they work so well. Pick a few of these and come back to this list to try them all at some point to see for yourself:

Use acid to cut fatty foods
For example: Cheese with Gewürztraminer [Guh-VERTZ-tra-meen-er] or Riesling

You have many options when pairing wine and cheese, and no single wine is right for every cheese, just as no single cheese would be right for every wine. But Gewürztraminer and Riesling are two good options for a wide variety of cheese pairings. They both offer predominant ripe tropical fruit flavors (think mangos, peaches, apricots) to offer broad partnership. Riesling generally has more acid to cut especially fatty cheeses, but Gewürztraminer has a floral aroma that will enliven your nose.

Strike a balance between similarities and differences
For example: Raw oysters and Muscadet [Moos-kah-DAY]

Muscadet is a wine from France's Western Loire Valley, roughly the central point in the country's stony Atlantic coast, comprised entirely of the Melon de Bourgogne [Mel-OWN duh boar-GOAN], aka Melon Blanc, grape. The wine is light to medium-bodied with neutral fruit and typically unoaked, though often left *sur lie*, meaning in contact with the yeast cells leftover from its production, for a few weeks before bottling. This provides body and complexity. The stony, saline qualities of Muscadet's location are reflected in the wine and explain why it is such a perfect match for the briny minerality of oysters. Further, its neutral fruit avoids detracting from the rich, buttery taste of the oysters, while its acidity helps clear your palate for the next slurp. This pairing is so common in fact that in France you are likely to be served oysters with a small paper cup of Muscadet. This is not for drinking, but rather for pouring on your oysters, taking the place of the lemon wedge more common in the rest of the world.

 Be careful not to confuse Muscadet, a crisp, dry, highly acidic white wine of neutral fruit character, with the similarly named Muscat [Moos-KAHT], an intense, overtly sweet almost syrupy white wine which would be an absolutely terrible pairing with oysters.

Use bubbles to cleanse your palate of strongly flavored foods
For example: Caviar and Champagne

Get fancy with us for a moment. Caviar and Champagne is a match made in gilded heaven. Caviar is incredibly salty, and without an appropriate beverage to accompany will soon fatigue your palate, dulling your senses to its nuances after just a few bites. The bubbles and acidity in Champagne are the perfect palate cleanser to help you enjoy each bite of caviar as if it were your first. Furthermore, the yeasty bread notes of the Champagne support the delicate brininess of the caviar much like a cracker.

> To learn more about Champagne and other sparkling wines, check out any of the *three* sparkling wine activities later in the book.

Contrast sweet and savory
For example: Fois gras with Sauternes [Saw-TURN]

> The **All For Dessert Wine** activity later in the book gives you the opportunity to enjoy several different styles of sweet wines.

Here's a pairing that's simply too rich to enjoy on your own, so be sure to invite some friends to join in the gluttony. Fois gras is just about the fattiest food you can eat outside of a stick of butter, and even the smallest bit demands a wine of equal weight and a sweetness to provide contrast. Fortunately the French long since solved this problem, and a Sauternes from Bordeaux provides the perfect blend of rich, sweet, dried fruits (think golden raisins and honey) to tempt your palate for another bite of ludicrously decadent fois. If enjoyed at home, you'll likely have plenty of Sauternes left after the fois gras is gone, so be sure to save some for dessert. It holds its own against sweet food and would pair especially well with mixed berries or cheesecake.

Remember, wine is fruit
For example: Duck and Pinot Noir

Have you ever wondered why so many duck dishes are served with fruit such as cherries or oranges (eg: Duck L'Orange?) It's because they taste like wine! At its core, wine is simply aged grapes, and keeping this basic point in mind lends to excellent pairings where the wine is treated as a side dish to accompany the main course. As restaurateur Danny Meyer has said: "People make such a big deal out of wine, but it's a condiment. It's a sauce to make the food taste better." Duck or Salmon with Pinot Noir (especially a fruit-forward Pinot Noir from the new world such as the widely available Benton Lane from Oregon) are perfect examples. The rich, fatty gaminess of the duck is enlivened by the bright red fruit character of the wine. No cherries needed!

> Check out the **All For Pinot Noir** activity later in the book to experience the difference between an old world and a new world Pinot Noir.

<u>Contrast sweet and spicy to keep your taste buds lively</u>
For example: Chinese takeout and Riesling

Have a look at the **All For Riesling** activity later in the book to learn more about why spicy Asian food pairs so well with the different styles of Rieslings.

Consider this the opposite of the caviar and fois gras pairings above! Get yourself a few dishes from your favorite inexpensive Chinese takeout restaurant and don't be shy about getting them spicy. Stir fry, fried rice and even General Tso's chicken are all well suited to a wine that offers enough sweetness to match the full flavors of the food. Off-dry (meaning slightly sweet) whites with minimal oak treatment such as Riesling or Muscat are great pairings with spicy Asian cuisine. Red wine is a little more difficult as you'll want to avoid tannins that clash with spicy flavors, but light-bodied fruity reds such as Gamay or anything from the southern Rhône Valley including Grenache [Gren-AWSH] and Syrah would work well. In all cases, consider the sweetness of the wines as a contrast to the spiciness of the food that will make the flavors of both the food and the wine dance on your tongue with every bite.

<u>Match intensities</u>
For example: Saucy Texas-style American BBQ with full-bodied off-dry reds, such as Zinfandel (ZIN-fan-del), or vinegary Carolina-style American BBQ with rosé, such as White Zinfandel

It's not enough to only match flavors. A perfect pairing will also consider the intensity of the food and beverage, and the different styles of American BBQ offer a telling comparison. For Texas-style BBQ that tends to be covered in sweet, sticky red sauce, look for a wine that will provide that same level of weighty texture and mouth feel. A full-bodied off-dry (slightly sweet) red such as new world Zinfandel is a great choice. Look out especially for anything by Joel Gott, considered the father of California Zinfandel. American Zinfandels tend to be incredibly powerful with plenty of rich sweetness (think dark chocolate and cherry jam) to stand up to that powerful sauce.

For Carolina-style American BBQ that tends to be more vinegary and peppery, you'll need to tone down the overt power and look for a wine that's lighter and crisper. Something with sweetness to contrast the BBQ, like a fruit punch, but with an edge of freshness to match the vinegar. A well-chilled rosé is a perfect accompaniment with just the right weight and sweetness to match the food, and this is one of the very few instances where we'd actually recommend a White Zinfandel pairing. White Zinfandel is rosé made from the same grapes as the red Zinfandel, but the process to produce the wine is drastically different and thus results in a pink wine with nearly opposite character. Now be warned, as if you won't look silly enough to your friends bringing wine to a BBQ, you are going to have an even bigger target on your back when you show up with a bottle of *pink* wine. Let them tease you and give you a hard time, as long as they promise to give it a try. And why shouldn't they? After all, pink wine has alcohol in it, and you brought it – who's going to say no to free alcohol at a BBQ?

White Zinfandel has a checkered history and many consider it an unsophisticated wine for novice consumers. But don't let that dissuade you from trying it out with BBQ some time! The sweet style of White Zinfandel sold today began as a mistake – a botched recipe – by the Sutter Home winery in 1975. But they sold it anyway, and when they found the resulting bottles flew off the shelves and consumers demanded more, they soon realized they had stumbled onto a hit: an easy drinking, sweet, pink wine. Sutter Home quickly expanded their White Zinfandel line and soon became one of the most successful sellers of inexpensive bulk wine in the country. The growing popularity of California White Zinfandel in the 1970s and 80s had the side effect of saving the Zinfandel vines that may have otherwise been pulled up and replaced with more popular varieties of the time. As tastes have come full circle, these old vines are now being used once again to produce high quality red Zinfandel, a wine that benefits greatly when produced from grapes off of older vines. Connoisseurs value and are willing to pay high prices for such wines. So next time you see an expensive bottle of California red Zinfandel on the top shelf of your local wine store, remember that it may own its very existence to that inexpensive box of White Zinfandel sitting down on the floor.

When in doubt, pair food with wine from the same region
For example: Red sauce pasta and a medium-bodied Italian red with low tannin such as Chianti [Kee-YAWN-tee]

Here's a strategy that works every time and will instantly transport you to any wine-growing region around the world. Simply pair food and wine from the same area. For example, Italian wine with pizza or pasta, Spanish wine with jamón ibérico or paella, French wine with camembert or duck cassoulet. The possibilities are not only endless, you can look for guidance online or by speaking with friends who have travelled to these countries to learn what the locals do. This strategy works especially well if you have a specialty store near you that focuses on a particular cuisine. Now you'll need to apply some basic logic to find a sensible pairing, especially in the case of a blind buy, but use the guidelines above such as matching the wine to the weight of the dish to be most successful. And don't hesitate to describe your meal to your local wine merchant to ask for their recommendation. In most cases they will have tried many of the wines in their store and will be able to point you to a specific bottle that will work best. And for an added dose of virtual jet-setting, kick off your meal by learning to say "cheers" in the region you've selected using the table on page 1!

Pair tannins with meat fats
For example: Marbled steak and Cabernet Sauvignon

This pairing is so good it's almost single-handedly responsible for the proliferation of high-end steak restaurants across the country. Quality red meat is full of earthy flavor that pairs beautifully with the tannins found in Cabernet Sauvignon. A well-marbled steak will have an even distribution of fat throughout the meat that will keep you sipping wine before and after every bite because the grip of the tannins so perfectly contrasts with the moist tenderness of the fat. If you are going to splurge on a nice piece of meat, you should have a wine that's up to the task, and this pairing works especially well with a Cabernet Sauvignon from Napa California that will have not only the tannins and structure to hold up to the fatty steak, but a lush fruitiness that will contrast with and thus highlight the meat's earthiness and rich beef flavor.

The **All For Cabernet Sauvignon & Merlot** activity later in this book will take you through another opportunity to pair Cabernet Sauvignon with a great steak.

Steak and red wine is also another example of using a wine's acid to cut through the food's fat, just like we saw with the Riesling and cheese above.

<u>Think of wine as the dessert, and find a food to accompany</u>
For example: Blue cheese (especially Stilton) and Port

Dessert pairings can be difficult since the food is usually selected first and thus your choice of wine is limited to those handful that can hold up to the sugar. As an alternative, take the opposite approach and select your wine first and plan your meal such that the wine is providing the sweetness and then find food that will match. A classic example is Port with blue cheese, in particular Ruby Port (as opposed to Tawny Port) with Stilton. Ruby Port is younger than Tawny Port and has retained more of its fruity grape characteristic. Tawny Port has spent more time in barrels and thus takes on more of an aged caramel flavor. Both wines are great, but in this case the fruit-forward Ruby Port pairs best with the salty creaminess of the blue cheese. Stilton is the blue cheese of choice here not just because of tradition, but because it is of high quality and has evenly dispersed veins so you are sure to get a bit of that salty tang in every bite. The richness of this pairing makes for a great winter-time dessert.

Discovering new pairings on your own
Now that we've explained why wine pairs so well with food and guided you through a few classic pairings to get you started, it's your turn to experiment and find great new pairings to share with your friends. A few guidelines to help you along the way:

<u>Balancing Act</u>
At its core, finding a good pairing of food and wine is about striking a balance between their similarities and their differences. You want to find foods and wines that are similar enough so as not to overwhelm each other or mask their delicacies, but different enough so as to highlight the best qualities of each.

Don't be afraid to venture far outside the box. Try to find a wine to pair with a cuisine that doesn't usually feature the beverage. Mexican or southern fried chicken for example. We've even heard of successful junk food pairings! Popeyes and Prosecco anyone?

<u>Match strong with strong, light with light</u>
This goes far beyond simply pairing whites with fish and reds with meat. In fact, some whites pair amazingly well with chicken and pork, and some lighter reds pair perfectly with tuna steak. Move beyond such strict limitations and instead think about matching strong food with strong wine, and light food with light wine. Consider not just the taste of your food and wine, but also the feel, weight and volume. For example, you might try pairing a wine with an oily, fatty texture such as Viognier with heavier dishes including cream sauce. The table below provides some guidelines:

	Lighter, Softer, Quieter, More Delicate	⬅ ➡	Heavier, Bigger, Louder, Stronger, Fuller
Ingredients	Fish Shellfish Vegetables	Pork Poultry Veal	Beef Game Lamb
Sauces	Citrus Vinaigrette	Butter or cream Olive oil	Meat stock Demi-glace
Techniques	Boiling Steaming Poaching	Baking Sautéing Roasting	Grilling Braising Stewing
Wines	<u>Whites</u> Muscadet Pinot Grigio / Pinot Gris Riesling Vinho Verde <u>Reds</u> Beaujolais Dolcetto Pinot Noir <u>Alcohol</u> < 12 percent	<u>Whites</u> Chardonnay (unoaked) Sauvignon Blanc <u>Reds</u> Barbera Chianti Classico Merlot <u>Alcohol</u> = 12-13 percent	<u>Whites</u> Chardonnay (oaked) Pinot Gris Viognier White Burgundy <u>Reds</u> Barolo Cabernet Sauvignon Shiraz / Syrah Zinfandel <u>Alcohol</u> > 13-14 percent

For more information on this endlessly fascinating topic of food and beverage pairings, check out the classic book *What to Drink with What You Eat* by Andrew Dornenburg and Karen Page.

A Blind Tasting Party

Level		Bottles		Price	**$$$$**

Wines to Buy:	We recommend five bottles, but this can be tailored to however many wines you'd like to try. If hosting a party, plan for one bottle for every two people. Wines of the same grape varietal or region that have differing price points work best. For example: all California Cabernets or all wines from Bordeaux at ~$10/under, ~$15, ~$20, ~$30 and splurge on a $50 bottle. We suggest sticking with red wines in this activity as they typically offer a wider variety of characteristics that may spark more debate. For the expert tasters out there, you can tailor the activity by choosing different expressions of the same grape: an Italian Barolo compared to a Barbaresco and a more generic Langhe Nebbiolo for example. This can be interesting as all three wines are produced in the Piedmont region in Italy and use the Nebbiolo grape, but differ in aging and other requirements (and price!). Another interesting activity may involve the same grape from different regions of the world, such as a California Cabernet Sauvignon, an Australian Cabernet and a French Bordeaux (make sure the Bordeaux is predominately Cabernet). Or even different vintages of wine from the same producer if you really want to challenge yourselves. The sky's the limit!
Other Items Needed:	A sheet of paper or newspaper to cover each bottle, a blank sheet of paper and pen for each person tasting, water, a neutral food like crackers or bread to cleanse the palate and plenty of friends.
What to Expect:	Can you really tell the difference between a $10 bottle of Yellowtail and a fine Barolo? Does not knowing the price of a wine increase or decrease your enjoyment? With this activity, find out which of your friends have Champagne tastes and which are cheap dates!

If you're like us, before you purchase a bottle of wine you usually read the back of the bottle, have asked for a recommendation or in some way done research on the wine. As you should! Making a blind buy can lead to disappointment, but a blind wine tasting can be quite enlightening.

The setup
This should be a blind tasting for everyone involved, so follow these two simple steps to make sure no one knows the true identity of the bottles:

1. Have one person cover each bottle of wine with a sheet of paper, newspaper or a brown paper bag while no one else is looking. Make sure the label is fully covered!
2. While no one else is looking, have a *different* person shuffle the bottles around and label each A, B, C, etc.

	Tasting Notes	Score	Est. Price
Bottle A			
Bottle B			
Bottle C			

With the bottles arranged, give every person a blank piece of paper and a pen. Down the left side of the page write the list of bottles you'll be tasting: A, B, C, etc. Across the top of the page write columns for tasting notes, a score from 1-4 stars and an estimated price.

And now you're ready to pour! With so many bottles it's unlikely you have enough glasses to pour everything for everyone at the start, so instead each taster will need just one glass. If you have enough wine glasses, also set out one reference glass per bottle. We'll use these for a visual and olfactory comparison across all the bottles. Start by pouring a small amount of each wine into the reference glasses. Then pour everyone a glass of the bottle labeled A.

The tasting

Appearance

Use the reference glasses to look at each of the wines. How do they differ in appearance?
Is one darker than another?
What would this indicate to you about how that wine is likely to taste?

If you are using wines that are the same grape variety and region (California Cabernets for example), the wines should look fairly similar with perhaps some variation depending on the age of the wine. Older wines tend to be a little lighter with a bit more color dispersion around the edges.

Smell

Sticking with the reference glasses for now, taking each in turn, swirl the first wine around in the glass and take a deep breath. What do you smell with each?
Are you getting certain fruits or floral notes, or maybe you smell minerals and earthiness, or maybe something different altogether?
Based on aroma alone, do you already have an early favorite?

Taste

Now turn your attention back to the glass of bottle A in front of you. Take a sip. Pause to collect your thoughts on the wine. The activity works best if each person jots a few notes on each wine for discussion and comparison later. Before you move on to the next wine, make sure you cleanse your palate thoroughly with water or bread in between so as not to obscure the results. How is the second wine different?
Is one more balanced than the other?
After you take a sip, pause for a bit and see how long the flavors of the wine linger. Does one have a longer finish?
Which do you think is the more expensive wine, and more importantly, which wine do you prefer?

The reveal

After you've gone through all the wines, discuss among the group. Revisit the wines as needed. Did everyone prefer the same wine, or does one of your friends have a wildly different palate?

After everyone has ranked the wines in order of preference and given their best guess on the price of each, it's time for the big reveal! How do everyone's wine preferences match up with their real price points?

If you're the cheap date of the bunch, consider yourself lucky! This activity may also help you determine what you value when considering wine. If you like the $20 bottle just as well as the $50 one, keep that in mind with your next purchase.

This is the first of three sparkling wine activities and you have several options for tackling these. First, you can take them as three separate activities and enjoy exactly as laid out in the pages that follow. We recommend this approach if you will be enjoying these activities with one to four people. An alternative is to combine the first two activities covering four bottles: one Champagne or Crémant or sparkling Californian wine from one of the major French producers, along with one Cava, one Prosecco and one Asti. We recommend this approach if you will be enjoying this activity with a group of four to eight people. A third option is to combine all three activities, which covers the above plus an additional bottle of either Champagne or Cava with different sweetness levels (see the **Sweetness Levels in Sparkling Wine** *activity for an explanation of what to look for). We recommend this approach if you will be hosting a party of eight or more people.*

Introduction to Champagne and the Champagne Method

Level	Bottles	Price
		$$$$

Wines to Buy:	For this activity you'll need two bottles of wine:
	1. The first should be a true Champagne, meaning a sparkling wine from the Champagne region of France. Such wines carry a significant premium over other sparkling wines because of their region of origin, but entry level bottles can be found for $40.
	2. For the second bottle you have two options. You can find a bottle of Crémant [cray-MAWN], which is a French sparkling wine made in the style of Champagne from other regions in France. Good examples can be found for under $20. You can also look for a sparkling wine from California produced by one of the major French Champagne houses such as Roederer Estate by Louis Roederer or Domaine Chandon by Möet et Chandon, both of which can be had for around $20, half the cost of their French counterparts.
	All sparkling wine should be served well-chilled, so get your bottles in the refrigerator at least three hours before you plan on serving. If you don't have that much time, you can chill a bottle in as little as 15 minutes by wringing out a wet paper towel and wrapping it around a bottle before placing it in the freezer. Once you've opened a bottle it's best to partially submerge it in a bowl of water and ice to keep it as cold as possible.
What to Expect:	Have you ever wondered why Champagne demands such a price premium over other sparkling wines? Or why it's often reserved for special occasions? This activity will describe how Champagne and wines produced in the "Champagne-method" are made. We'll walk you through a detailed tasting of Champagne, pointing out its unique characteristics that differentiate it from other sparkling wines, along with another wine produced in the same method but selling for half the price. By the end of this activity you'll be armed with all the knowledge you need to find a perfect bottle of sparkling wine for that special occasion, without breaking the bank.

As you've no doubt gathered by now, not all sparkling wine is Champagne! It's a testament to the long history and high quality of Champagne that its name has become synonymous with sparkling wine of any type, but the term Champagne precisely refers to a *specific* style of sparkling wine, made from *specific* grapes with a *specific* technique from a *specific* region in France. *Whew!*

 It's exciting to open a bottle of sparkling wine, with its distinctive popping sound and outpouring of bubbles it's a sure sign you are ready to party. But these bottles can be dangerous – the pressure inside a sparkling wine bottle is four times the air pressure in a car tire – and drinking is a lot less fun if someone gets hurts or you have to clean up half a bottle of spilled wine off the floor. In other words, resist the temptation to open a bottle like you just won The World Series. Instead, follow these simple steps to make sure you stay safe and have a full bottle to enjoy: 1) sparkling wine is less volatile when chilled, so be sure the bottle is nice and cold before opening, 2) once you've removed the wire basket from the top of the bottle keep your thumb on top of the cork at all times or place a hand towel over the bottle, 3) while holding the cork steady, slowly twist the bottle to release the cork as gently as possible, 4) slowly pour the wine into tall glasses to preserve (and show off!) those beautiful bubbles.

Champagne

Let's start with the Champagne. Only sparkling wine made from Pinot Noir, Chardonnay and/or Pinot Meunier [PEE-no min-ur] grapes in the Champagne region of Northern France may be labeled as such. But the method used to create Champagne can be used by anyone, which is why the label on your other bottle may say "méthode Champenoise" or "in the Champagne method." So what does this mean? Well there are many subtle differences in the Champagne method of production, but the one we will focus on here is that the secondary fermentation occurs in the bottle, rather than in tanks as is done with most other sparkling wines, most notably Prosecco, which you'll try in the next activity.

All wines go through a fermentation process that turns sugar and yeast into alcohol and carbon dioxide. This process takes place in large open vats that allow the carbon dioxide to release into the air, while the alcohol remains in the liquid that is now becoming wine. To produce a sparkling wine, winemakers run an existing still white wine through a second fermentation that this time captures that carbon dioxide under pressure, producing bubbles. In Champagne, this secondary fermentation takes place over a period of at least 12 months in the bottle itself rather than a large vat. This prolonged contact of wine and yeast in the tight confines of the bottle can yield extraordinary results.

Pour a glass, and as you taste the wine see if you can identify the savory bready flavors of dough and biscuit that this prolonged yeast exposure has contributed. Does this wine feel rich and decadent, almost like a meal in itself? Is this breadiness complemented by toasty brioche aromas and flavors?

As you continue sipping the Champagne, look for other flavors. How would you describe the fruit and accompanying acidity? If it were an apple, would you say that it tastes more like a bruised or baked yellow apple than a fresh green apple?

Consider also the minerality of the wine. Due to the Champagne region's unique soil many people detect a pleasant chalkiness to the wines which may come across in the texture as much as the taste. Does "chalky" sound like the right word to describe your wine?

Finally, regarding the texture, consider how the bubbles feel in your mouth. Quality Champagnes have a silky texture due to the fine beads (small bubbles) that enhance the sweet and savory flavors of the wine as they burst in your mouth. With your next sip see if you can feel the bubbles and describe how they feel in relation to bubbles in soda or carbonated water. Hint: they better feel a lot smaller and more refined for the price you paid for this bottle!

 Refer to the bubbles as "beads" to sound like a real expert. For example – "This champagne has such a fine bead" would mean the bubbles are small. You can also refer to the overall fizziness of the wine as the "mousse." A tight mousse feels dense yet soft in the mouth and will form a visible layer of foam when poured into a glass; whereas a loose mousse feels pronounced and harsh, like soda fresh from the can and will not form that layer of foam.

Let's delve a little deeper into the specifics of the bottle in front of you. When it comes to grape composition, Champagne comes in three varieties. A Champagne made with only Chardonnay is called a "blanc de blancs", meaning "white from white", while one made from Pinot Noir and/or Pinot Meunier is called a "blanc de noir", meaning "white from black." The third option is the most common and is wine made from blending all three grapes. If your bottle doesn't clearly state "blanc de blanc" or "blanc de noir", it's most likely a blend exhibiting characteristics of both.

 That's not a typo – white wine can be made from red grapes such as Pinot Noir. Red wine gets its color from the skins of the grape, not the flesh. Extracting the juice from red grapes with minimal skin contact is a delicate process and one of the many reasons Champagne-style wines are difficult and expensive to produce.

The resulting wines will express characteristics of their grapes. The blanc de blanc will be whiter, have greater minerality and ultimately more finesse. Classic food pairings abound and reflect the decadence of the wine: caviar, oysters and lobster are all perfect accompaniments. Compared to the blanc de blanc, the blanc de noir will have a slightly deeper color, though still pale and very much a white wine, and a more red fruit (think cherries) and earth-driven character with greater power. Blanc de noirs offer intriguing food pairings that straddle the line between typical white and red wines. Veal, salmon and even duck would be excellent pairings. Blended Champagnes are equally delicious and offer the broadest range of food pairings.

Crémant or Champagne-style California wine

Now that you've dedicated proper attention to the Champagne, let's move to its less-expensive counterpart which will be either the Crémant or Champagne-style California wine. Crémant is a French sparkling wine made in the style of Champagne from other regions in France. Its region of origin will typically be indicated on the label such as "Crémant d'Alsace" or "Crémant de Bordeaux." While such wines may be produced anywhere in France, and from a wider variety of grapes than Champagne, they must be produced using the same in-bottle secondary fermentation method that supplies the bready, yeasty flavors you enjoyed in the Champagne.

The Champagne-style California wine is a similar story. Different region and possibly different grapes, but same technique. In fact, despite being produced thousands of miles from France, California wine produced by French houses Roederer, Chandon, Mumm and others may be even more similar to their Champagne counterparts than competing Crémants given their common corporate parentage.

Compare the aroma and taste of this second bottle to the Champagne. Do you detect the same doughy brioche notes, or are you picking up something else instead? In the case of California wines in particular you may find that the fruit dominates, owing to the ripeness of the growing environment.

How about the minerality? You'll likely find that this wine lacks the pleasant chalky quality of the Champagne, but does it even come close?

Thinking more about the texture, this wine likely does share the Champagne's creamy mouthfeel and tight bead, both of which are hallmarks of high-quality sparkling wine that any producer will strive for. Can you feel any difference at all?

Once you are done with your glass, revisit the Champagne. The comparison should help you find some of the more subtle nuances of the Champagne. Look for the chalky minerality, the toasted brioche flavors and the fine bead that melts on your tongue.

Conclusion

Now that you've experienced a true Champagne alongside its similar counterparts, what's your conclusion? Price aside, which did you prefer? It's not uncommon to actually prefer the non-Champagne! Keep in mind, real estate is extraordinarily expensive in the Champagne region and this cost is reflected in the bottle. In the $40 price range you are drinking an entry-level Champagne which may not compare as favorably to a less expensive but high-quality regional alternative.

Even if you do prefer the Champagne, does it justify the higher price? In the end, even if we can argue about whether Champagne is worth the lofty price tag, do you think it deserves its place atop the beverage pyramid? In our mind, quality Champagne is an impeccable example of terroir, grapes and production method perfectly complementing each other. The region has a cool climate far enough north so as to produce grapes with the acidity to balance a high level of sweetness. The rich Chardonnay and fruity, earthy Pinot Noir grapes form a complex blend. And, the high-quality production technique that introduces savory, bready characteristics with a fine, creamy bead all come together perfectly to produce a beverage worthy of celebration.

Perhaps the world's most famous Champagne is Dom Pérignon. Somewhat less famous is the 17th century French Benedictine monk after whom the wine is named, Dom Pierre Pérignon, who served at the Abbey of Saint Peter of Hautvillers in Northeast France. Myth and marketing surround the legend of the man, but historical evidence points to his early advocacy of organic wine-making techniques and his authorship of a set of wine-making rules that set the standard for decades to come. Known as a perfectionist with an exceptional palate, his wine was highly regarded throughout Europe as a superior and well-balanced product that became a favorite of King Louis XIV (the "Sun King"). However, what's not mentioned in the all the marketing hoopla is that Dom Pérignon produced red wine, not white, and certainly not the Champagne style sparkling wine we associate with him today. In fact, back in the 17th century the last thing Dom Pérignon would have wanted in his wines were fermentation bubbles for the very practical reason that such bottles were prone to exploding in the cellar! Without the modern bottling techniques we take for granted today, sparkling wines at the time were considered a mistake and a nuisance best avoided. They were such a problem that cellar workers routinely wore metal masks to protect their faces from shards of flying glass from bottles that had accidentally fermented. No wonder they don't mention this in the marketing!

Other Styles of Sparkling Wine

Level		Bottles	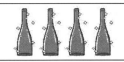	Price	

Wines to Buy:	You'll need four bottles of sparkling wine for this activity so it's a great opportunity to invite your friends over for a party. Ideally one bottle will be a Champagne, Crémant, or a sparkling wine from California produced by one of the major French Champagne houses (see the **Introduction to Champagne** activity immediately preceding this one). In addition to this, you'll want a bottle of Cava, a bottle of Prosecco and a bottle of Asti [AH-stee], also known as Asti Spumante [Spoo-MAWN-tay], each of which need not cost more than $12. As always, all sparkling wine should be served well-chilled.
What to Expect:	This activity is a face-off between Champagne and other sparkling wines from France (Crémant), Spain (Cava) and Italy (Prosecco and Asti). You'll learn how each is produced differently and why this contributes to their flavors and price.

The predominant flavors of sparkling wine are determined more by the production method than the grapes (in fact most sparkling wine producers don't even list the grape varieties on the bottle), and each of the four bottles you've gathered for this activity was produced using a different method. While there is no single "best" method for producing sparkling wine, there are methods that work better given the terroir and grape varieties available to each producer, and for this reason the method used in production typically coincides with a region of the world.

Among the many methods used to produce sparkling wines, you will see that none of these are carbonated through carbon dioxide injection like sodas. Beverages carbonated by injection are inexpensive to produce but contain large bubbles that mask delicate flavors and quickly lose their fizz — consider how quickly an open can of soda goes flat. Not exactly what you want with your wine. So with your friends gathered, your bottles popped and this introductory information behind us, let's find something to toast and have a drink!

Champagne

The name Champagne has in many ways become synonymous with quality, elegance and sophistication, but is it really worth the premium? Are the beads really finer, the acidity really brighter, and the texture really smoother? See the **Introduction to Champagne** activity to learn more about the Champagne method of production. If combining these activities, no need to purchase both a Champagne and a Crémant or sparkling wine from California produced by one of the major French Champagne houses. Just one of the three will do.

Cava

Starting with Champagne may seem unfair to the rest of the bottles in front of you. But when it comes to Cava, value is the name of the game. For a bottle of wine that likely cost less than half or even a third of what you paid for the Champagne, the Cava, believe it or not, was made using the exact same in-bottle fermentation method. But there are important differences between the two.

Let's start with appearance. Looking at a glass of each, you may find that the Cava is paler than the Champagne, especially if your Champagne is a blanc de noir. This is because the vast majority of Cava is produced from several varieties of local Spanish grapes, all of which are white. Go ahead and take a sip of the Cava. Before we get to specific flavors, consider the acidity. You may find the Cava tastes less acidic. This is due to its region of origin. Nearly all Cava is produced in the Catalonia region of Northeast Spain bordering Southern France. While this is as far north you can go within Spain, it's still about 700 miles south of Champagne. This distance, combined with Catalonia's proximity to the Mediterranean Sea's warming influence, produces riper grapes that result in less acidic wine.

Now consider the actual flavors of the Cava. Whereas the Champagne had prominent savory biscuit flavors, you likely find the Cava to have a more straightforward citrus character. Think dense, chewy lemons. This reduced bready complexity is due to the Cava having spent less time in contact with the yeast in the bottle. Even though it follows the same in-bottle fermentation process as Champagne, the aging requirement is shorter and Cava is typically released to the market sooner than a Champagne that began production at the same time.

Comparing the two side by side, what other aromas and flavors do you find in the Cava?
Perhaps pear and melon notes, or even hints of flowers?
With the Cava offering a point of comparison, are you also now finding aromas and flavors in the Champagne that you didn't detect before?
You may also find the Cava has a slightly bitter finish, like a green almond. Some people like this, while others find it leaves them with an unpleasant aftertaste.
Consider also the texture of the Cava. Would you describe it as creamy like the Champagne, or is it frothier?

So which is better? Well, the Champagne may offer higher acidity and more savory complexity, but this isn't best for every occasion. The lush, ripe grapes in the Cava may pair better with hearty fare, especially traditional Spanish dishes such as Jamón ibérico and paella. It is also a great accompaniment to rich seafood dishes like fried fish, salmon or tuna sushi. Cava is also perfect for parties given its similarity to Champagne at a much lower price that makes bulk buying easier on the wallet.

Prosecco

Now we're moving on to an entirely different beast altogether. Whether you realize it or not, you've probably had a lot more Prosecco in your life than either Champagne or Cava. Those "champagne toasts" at New Year's parties and weddings, bellinis and mimosas at brunch, even that bottle you brought to your friend's housewarming party – odds are those were all Proseccos. Prosecco is perfect for many occasions due to its lower price, but it's not just a cheap alternative to Champagne. It has its own charms and is a great style of sparkling wine in its own right.

Have a sip and see if you agree that of the three wines tasted so far the Prosecco is the freshest and most plainly fruit-driven. Do you detect notes of peaches or other stone fruits? Unlike Champagne and Cava, Prosecco's secondary fermentation does not take place in the bottle. Instead it takes place in large, pressurized vats, similar to the open vats used during primary fermentation, but this time with the lid on. This pressurized fermentation is essentially a bulk version of the in-bottle fermentation of Champagne and Cava. This process is called the charmat [Shar-MAH] method of production, though this is rarely printed on the label since it's not a distinctive sign of high quality. Given this mass production, these wines will have less contact with the yeast that lends that bready character, and thus they will taste simpler with primary notes of citrus fruit and flowers without that toasty complexity. This is why the Prosecco probably tastes more like peaches and nectarines than the other wines in this activity. And you can see now why it makes such a natural pairing with brunch cocktails. Prosecco is intended to be enjoyed young while these fruit flavors are fresh and vibrant so it's rarely aged and is best consumed upon release.

Prosecco is honest in its simplicity. It's produced in the northwest region of Italy near Venice from a light, neutral white grape called Glera. The simple nature of the grape pairs perfectly with the production technique to produce a lightweight, frothy sparkling wine with a relatively larger bubble than those wines fermented in the bottle. With three glasses in front of you compare the color and mouse. Most likely the Prosecco is the palest of the three with the frothiest layer of foam resting on top.

After a sip of the Prosecco revisit the Champagne. If you weren't detecting those savory biscuit notes before they should be jumping out at you now.

Asti

And finally we come to Asti, which in some ways is the ugly duckling of this group, but has its merits.

Pour yourself a glass of Asti and first look at the wine. You'll likely see the Asti is beyond sparkling, it's frothy, a signature of Moscato. Smell the wine, noticing that more than any of the wines enjoyed so far this will smell like fresh white grape juice with intensely floral aromas of white flowers and honeysuckle. Taste the wine and see if you detect light, fruity flavors of peaches and white grapes. On the finish notice that this wine goes down easy with no burn in your throat, a telltale sign of low alcohol. Check the bottle to see if this is right – most Astis are closer to 6% alcohol compared to the 12% found in most other sparkling wines.

Asti is a sweet, fruity, light-bodied sparkling wine from the Piedmont region in Northwest Italy made from the Muscat grape. Asti is usually fully sparkling but may have less fizz than the other bottles you have open, especially if it's labeled Moscato d'Asti. Wines in this category are generally far lower in alcohol but much higher in sugar content than other sparkling wines. These are generally straightforward wines meant to be enjoyed without introspection so are great for casual parties where your attention is on enjoying good company rather than analyzing a wine's nuances. (Can you tell why we are drinking this bottle last?)

The production method for Asti is unusual amongst sparkling wines because there is only one fermentation. To make Asti, non-alcoholic white grape juice (not wine) is placed in a pressurized tank and yeast is added to start the fermentation. Initially the carbon dioxide is allowed to escape and it is only towards the end of the fermentation process that the carbon dioxide is trapped to achieve the desired level of carbonization. Once the yeast has had time to convert the sugar in the grape juice into the desired level of alcohol the fermentation process is halted by chilling the wine to very cold temperatures. The wine is then filtered to remove the yeast and bottled under pressure to preserve the bubbles. Note that this process avoids prolonged contact with the yeast so the resulting wine will be fresh and simple.

Conclusion

By now you've enjoyed four distinct glasses of sparkling wine, and are probably having a very good time. Were you able to detect the major differences and similarities in each bottle? The look, aroma, taste and feel (mousse)? Take a moment to reflect on each.

Did you prefer the savory character of the Champagne or the fruitiness and floral notes of the Prosecco?

Did you detect any difference between the Champagne and the similarly-produced Cava?

What did you make of the fruity, low-alcohol Asti?

Did you have a single overall preference, or do you find that they each have their place?

Which would you pair with an upscale dinner, a summer afternoon picnic with family or a new year's celebration with friends?

Regardless of which wine you liked best overall, we think you'll find they each have their place and can be enjoyed under various circumstances.

Sweetness Levels in Sparkling Wine

Level		Bottles		Price	

Wines to Buy:	You'll need three bottles of sparkling wine that represent various levels of sweetness as indicated by their official designation (eg: Extra Brut, Semi-dry, Sweet, etc.). One of the bottles should have "Brut" in the name, one should be "Dry" or "Extra-Dry" and one should either be "Semi-dry" or have "Sweet" in the name. Refer to the grid on page 50 for more details and aim to span as wide a range as possible. These terms will be displayed very clearly on the front of the bottle as key descriptors for any sparkling wine. A Brut Nature Champagne, an Extra Dry Cava or Prosecco and a Sweet Asti would be an ideal lineup, but a more economical approach would substitute an Extra Brut Cava for the Champagne.
	Be sure to serve well-chilled and if possible use a different glass for each wine so by the end of the activity everyone will have a glass of each in front of them to aid comparison.
What to Expect:	Sweetness level is the single most important attribute of any sparkling wine. In this activity we'll demystify the terms "Brut" and "Dry", provide some historic context, walk through the full spectrum of sweetness levels, help you discover the wine that perfectly suits your taste and arm you with the knowledge and experience to select the right bottle for any occasion.

If you've completed the **Introduction to Champagne** or **Other Styles of Sparkling Wine** activities earlier in this book you will recall that most sparkling wines are produced by sending still wine through a secondary fermentation process, either in the bottle itself as with Champagne and Cava, or in large vats as with Prosecco. This process and the resulting "disgorgement" (removal of residual yeast following aging) allow winemakers to make additional changes to the wine before final bottling. One of the key alterations at this stage is a process called "dosage" where winemakers add a small amount of sugar syrup to the wine to create the desired sweetness. However, the perceived sweetness of sparkling wine is entirely relative to its acid levels. Given most base wines used to make sparkling wines are naturally high in acid, even those with added sugar syrup can taste bone dry as the acid negates the taste of the sugar. This is key to the art of winemaking as the producer takes an underlying still wine and uses the precise dosage to create the perfect end product that matches their desired level of sweetness.

Brut
We'll work our way through each of your bottles starting with the driest (least amount of added sugar). Let's start with the Brut (Brut Nature, Extra Brut or Brut all work here). When enjoying multiple wines it's always best to start with the wine with the lowest sweetness and gradually work towards the highest sweetness. This will preserve your taste buds which are especially susceptible to sugar fatigue. Starting with the sweetest wines would overwhelm your taste buds causing you to miss the subtle flavors in the subsequent drier wines.

Pour everyone a glass and find something to toast! Before we start paying attention to flavors and acidity, use your first sip of wine to prepare your mouth to notice the subtleties we'll discuss in a moment. The first sip of any sparkling wine will taste overly citric and acidic simply because your mouth wasn't expecting it, so swish the wine around your entire mouth as a sort of primer.

With your next sip start to pay attention to your salivary glands. Is your mouth watering? With little to no sugar to counteract the acidity of the wine you may feel your salivary glands reacting for several seconds after you've swallowed the wine. This reaction is precisely why dry sparkling wine makes such a good aperitif – the acidity is opening your taste buds so you can more fully enjoy the meal to follow. Or in our case, the other wines to follow!

What do you make of this wine? Tastes great, right? It's hard to judge in isolation, so enjoy a few more sips and then move on to the next bottle as it will be easier to highlight their attributes through comparison.

 When French Champagne first became popular it was made as sweet as modern-day soda, and this was the preferred style until the mid-1800s. At that point, demand rose for less sweet versions and the term dry was created to describe these wines (implying something less sweet than soda at the time). As tastes continued to evolve and demand from international markets grew, preferences moved even further towards the drier end of the spectrum. Champagne needed new terminology to indicate "drier than dry." The term "brut" was created to connote the savage or harsh lack of sweetness. So when you see the term brut, just think "drier than dry."

Dry

And now as if the manufactured term "brut" weren't confusing enough, we come to the most misunderstood level of sweetness of all. Despite the name, when it comes to sparkling wines, dry actually means somewhat sweet. Reflect on the history of modern wine in the above Sidebar and the original use of the term dry to mean anything less sweet than soda and it makes perfect sense. But know that a dry sparkling wine will be sweeter than a dry still wine. To quantify this difference, according to European Union regulations a still wine labeled dry may have no more than four grams of residual sugar per liter. A dry sparkling wine *must have at least* 17 and *can have up to* 32 grams of residual sugar per liter! For perspective, a 12 ounce can of Coca Cola has 38 grams of sugar. So a standard 750 ml bottle of dry sparkling wine could have as much as half of a can of Coke's worth of sugar **_more_** than a bottle of dry still wine!

Pour everyone a glass of your extra dry or dry sparkling wine and have a sip. Do you immediately notice the extra sugar, or does it take some thought?

Don't worry if you don't taste the extra sugar. There are two major reasons why you may not notice the difference. First, despite the different names your brut and dry wines may have fairly similar levels of sugar. Find each of your wines on the sweetness scale on page 50. If your first glass was a brut and your second is an extra dry, your sugar levels could technically be identical at 12 grams per liter! You should notice much more of a difference if you are comparing a brut nature or extra brut with a dry wine. The other reason you may not detect the different levels of sweetness is that winemakers generally aim to produce balanced wines where high sugar content is offset by higher acidity. In your dry sparkling wine the sugar is there, you just may not taste it as much given the counter-balancing impact of the acid.

Sweet

Sweet sparkling wines sometimes don't get the same respect as their drier counterparts and are often relegated to picnics and bachelorette parties. But these wines have a lot going for them when paired with appropriate food. Pour everyone a glass and have a sip. Compared to the brut you should now really be noticing the different sugar levels. Even with all the sugar however, you should still find your wine remains in balance. A quality producer will balance the high sugar with equally high acid and aromatics.

Smell the wine and see if strong fruit or floral scents are as prominent on the nose as the sugar is on the palate. Also note the acidity. Again, the acidity should keep the higher sugar in check to produce a balanced result. No doubt this wine is on the sweeter end of the spectrum, but it shouldn't taste like soda.

This balance of sugar and acid makes sweet sparkling wine an ideal pairing for a highly-flavored meal (think very spicy or salty food such as Chinese takeout) because the sugar balances the extreme salt and spice while the acid and the mouth-watering result that follows will help wash away the flavor and prepare you to enjoy the next bite as if it were your first. A sweet sparkling Asti may be taking it a step too far and is best reserved for after a meal, but a semi-dry offering is a great match for General Tso's Chicken, Kung Pao Shrimp or Szechuan Wontons!

Bringing it Together
With three glasses now in front of you, take a moment to smell each wine. Can you smell the different level of sweetness in each? In fact you shouldn't be able to because sugar is odorless! If you don't believe us, pour a bit of sugar into a bowl and smell for yourself!

Now that you've sampled wines that span the sweetness spectrum, do you have a favorite?
Did you enjoy the bracing acidity of the brut, or was it too savage for your tastes?
Did you find the sweet wine was easier drinking and more your style, or was it too syrupy?
Or did you prefer the dry as a balanced combination of the two?

There is no wrong answer as it all comes down to your preferences and finding the right time and place for each wine. We find the driest sparkling wines are a great way to start an evening or enliven an appetizer course of a long meal. Wines in the middle of the spectrum are great for every day enjoyment, weekend brunch, casual partying and even mixing in cocktails (Bellinis, Mimosas, etc.) The sweetest sparkling wines are our favorites for ending a meal as an alternative to dessert, or pairing with berries. And when you're on a budget and need to please a crowd, there are inexpensive versions of each of these wines waiting to be purchased in bulk for your next birthday, New Year's party or wedding!

Sparkling Wine Sweetness Scale

Sweetness terms are governed by EU regulations but given they can be confusing we've decoded the terms below.

Official designation	Brut Nature	Extra Brut	Brut	Extra Dry, Extra Sec, Extra Seco	Dry, Sec, Seco	Semi-dry, Semi-seco, Demi-sec	Sweet, Doux, Dulce
Taste	Bone dry	Dry	Medium dry	Medium sweet	Sweet	Very sweet	Extremely sweet
Description	The sweetness of any of these wines will be imperceptible to all but those with the most trained palates. These are the wines to serve as an aperitif or to accompany a meal.			You should be able to taste the sweetness level in these wines. "Extra dry" is the most confusing term. Despite the name, "extra" in this case actually means less dry (ie: sweeter) than Brut.		Wines in these categories will taste overtly sweet. These are the wines to serve after a meal or with dessert.	
Residual sugar (grams / liter)	0-3 with no sugar added	0-6	0-12	12-17	17-32	32-50	> 50
Examples		Champagne					
			Cava				
				Prosecco			
							Asti

A Virtual Tour of the Rhône Valley

Level		Bottles		Price	

Wines to Buy:	You'll need two bottles. The first may be a splurge, but good values abound for the second bottle to make up for it. Sub-region aside, the most important aspect of your two bottles is the grape dominating the blend: for the Northern Rhône look for a wine comprised entirely or mostly of Syrah, for the Southern Rhône look for a wine comprised entirely or mostly of Grenache, the higher percentage of the primary grape the better in both instances. 1. A Syrah from the Northern Rhône: Rhône wines are categorized by sub-region where quality options include Côte Rôtie [Coat ro-TEE], Saint Joseph and Crozes-Hermitage [Crow-ZAY er-mi-TAHJ]. A good example of either of the first two may run you $40 or more, but a Crozes-Hermitage should be available for around $20. Chapoutier and Jaboulet are two reliable producers in this price range. 2. A Grenache from the Southern Rhône: Again categorized by region, a few options include Côtes du Rhône [Coat do ROW-n], Gigondes [Jhee-gone-DAS], Vinsobres [Vin-SOBE] and Châteauneuf-du-Pape [Shat-en-OOF du POP]. The Côtes du Rhône is an opportunity for an especially good value with many quality examples available for $15 or less. You may be hard-pressed to find a bottle from the Southern Rhône that's 100% Grenache since much of the wine from this area is a blend (more on this in a moment), and that's okay. To be certain your bottle will meet our needs check the label or ask your wine store to make sure that the Grenache dominates the blend.
What to Expect:	Take a virtual trip down France's Rhône Valley, one of the premiere wine-growing regions in the world. Here you'll learn the difference in climate, grapes and style between the Northern and the Southern Rhône while tasting such classic wines as Côte Rôtie, Côtes du Rhône, Châteauneuf-du-Pape and other "GSM blends" that dominate the region.

The Rhône Valley stretches for roughly 100 miles through Southeastern France from Vienne in the north to Avignon in the south, ending about 30 miles north of the Mediterranean Sea. A moderate climate dominates the area, but stark contrasts in topography, microclimates and wine laws result in drastically different styles of wine between the north and south. Go ahead and pour glasses of both wines as you'll want to be able to see, smell and tastes their differences side by side as we continue.

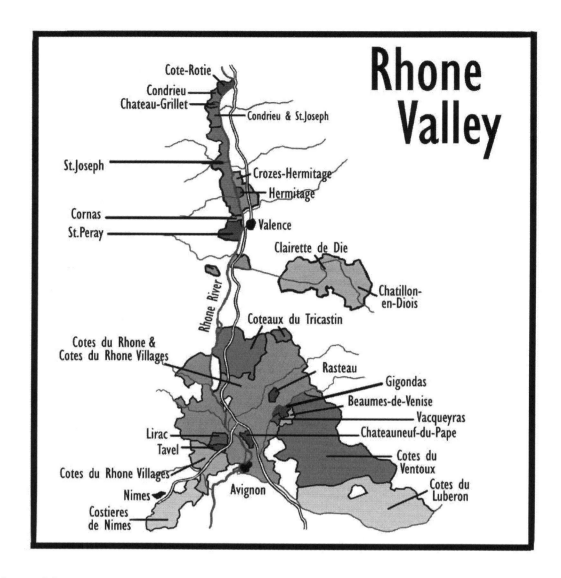

Northern Rhône

In the north, steep slopes lead down from the surrounding hills to the winding Rhône River below. The very best vineyards in the region will be on the southern side of these hills in order to capture the most sunlight throughout the day, a fact alluded to by the name of the north's premier appellation, Côte Rôtie, meaning "roasted slope." While good for the grapes, these steep slopes are not good for your wallet as the precariously terraced vineyards require expensive hand harvesting, the cost of which inevitably shows up in the price of the bottle. Compared to premium appellations such as Côte Rôtie and Saint Joseph, Crozes-Hermitage is located on flatter, easier to harvest land and is thus a relative value in the northern Rhône, though with some sacrifice of diminished flavors due to receiving less sun. If you are drinking a Côte Rôtie or Saint Joseph, relish in the prestige and history associated with your wine from one of the finest regions in the world. If you are drinking a Crozes-Hermitage, take pleasure in having found a relative bargain from an adjacent appellation.

Whatever bottle you ended up with, tilt your glass over a white surface and notice how dark the wine is, especially compared to the southern Rhône. Syrah is the only permitted red grape in the northern Rhône and its thick skins combined with the ripeness that develops from such intense sun produce a deeply-colored wine. Knowing this, without even smelling or tasting the wine you can probably already guess that it's going to be full-bodied with significant tannins.

Take a sniff. Anything jumping out at you? Black pepper aromas and flavors are the hallmark of moderate climate Syrah. If you are in a group and only some of you are getting this, don't worry – black pepper is in fact the single most common aroma blind-spot with as much as 20% of the population genetically unable to smell it. Other common aromas in Syrah include black fruit such as blackberries and dark cherries, herbaceous notes, licorice and even smoked meat and bacon.

Take a sip to see if the palate follows the aromas or you are finding additional nuance. Apart from the flavors above, a young Syrah will typically show some element of dark chocolate. An aged Syrah may produce notes of leather, earth and "forest floor", a common wine descriptor hinting at wet leaves, mushrooms or even truffles. Many of these wines are barreled in French oak, providing additional notes of toast, vanilla and coconut.

With a preference for extended intense sun exposure it's no surprise that Syrah has become the predominant grape in Australia. See the **All For Syrah/Shiraz** activity later in this book to learn more about the difference between the northern Rhône and Australian expressions of the grape.

Syrah is the only permitted red grape in the northern Rhône, and is only ever mixed with small amounts (no more than 20%) of the white grape Viognier [Vee-yo-NAY]. This unique blend of red and white grapes is especially popular in Côte Rôtie where the introduction of Viognier grapes during fermentation lends a smoother texture and exotic fruit notes to the resulting wine. If you enjoyed the Syrah you used in this activity, ask your local wine merchant for help finding a northern Rhône Syrah-Viognier blend and taste the difference. If you can't find an example from the northern Rhône, a suitable substitute may be found from California's Santa Barbara County, though keep in mind the difference between old and new world wine styles will make the comparison to your 100% Syrah from the Rhône more complicated.

Southern Rhône
Compared to the north, the southern Rhône has a slightly warmer climate and much flatter land, a combination producing ripe grapes without the need to hand harvest and thus a less expensive bottle of wine. A key feature of the southern Rhône is the wide variety of grapes available for blending, most prominently Grenache, Syrah and Mouvèdre [Moo-VEH-drah], often referred to as the "GSM blend." This blend is so popular you may even see just "GSM" printed on the label without even naming the grapes. Côtes du Rhône is one of the most famous sub-regions of the southern Rhône. Given its large size and perfect growing conditions, this is an area of particular value in French wine. If you ever find yourself roaming the aisles looking for a $10 wine for a casual dinner or to bring to a party, seek out a Côtes du Rhône to impress your friends and get bang for your buck.

Grenache is also widely grown in the Rioja [Ree-OH-ha] and Priorat [PROY-rot] regions of Spain where it is called Garnacha [Gar-NACH-ah]. The Priorat style is remarkably different than most other Grenache as the region's unique combination of old vines and steeply terraced land produces powerful wines that are richly concentrated with full tannins, closer to an inky Cabernet Sauvignon than a gentle Pinot Noir!

Since you've already tasted the northern Rhône wine you know the key elements of Syrah: deep color with medium or high tannin, dark fruits, chocolate and black pepper. Grenache is the opposite in nearly every way: it's lighter in color with less tannin and has notes of red fruits and white pepper. In fact, if you are having a bottle of 100% Grenache instead of a blend you might find that it reminds you of Pinot Noir as they are both generally light to medium-bodied wines with a similar aroma and flavor profile. The key flavor differences are that Grenache is typically higher in alcohol and lower in acidity.

Start by smelling your second glass of wine and consider how it compares to the first. Can you detect the lighter, red fruit aromas of the Grenache in the blend? Think strawberries and raspberries.

Have a sip. Compared to the Syrah, do you find it to be lighter-bodied? Does any of the black pepper flavor remain or has the Grenache smoothed that away?

 Grenache can age very well, taking on leather and toffee notes over time. While French versions can get enormously expensive, aged Grenache from major Australian producers such as Clarendon Hills and Penfolds can be found in the sub $30 range and is worth the occasional splurge.

As you continue comparing and contrasting the wines, be sure to check out the **All For Cabernet Sauvignon and Merlot** activity later in this book and consider the similarities of the Rhône's use of Syrah and Grenache to Bordeaux's use of Cabernet Sauvignon and Merlot. Syrah and Grenache form a remarkably similar pair where the Syrah provides the color, tannin, acidity and dark fruit character (like Cabernet Sauvignon) while Grenache provides the alcohol and softer red fruit character (like Merlot). The addition of Mouvèdre in small quantities can bring additional notes of sweet and savory spices along with dark chocolate.

So in the end what do you prefer? Do you like the full-bodied intensity of the Syrah from northern Rhône or the lighter red fruit flavors of the Grenache from the south? Or do you find that a GSM blend offered the best of both worlds? If you didn't have the opportunity to try a Côtes du Rhône as part of this activity, be sure to look for one the next time you are browsing the aisles of your local wine shop. They are immensely popular and typically a good value for the money. And once you start looking you'll find them everywhere. They are an especially common choice for wines served by the glass, be it at a wedding or on an international flight, so now you'll know what to expect.

A Virtual Tour of Piedmont

Level		Bottles		Price	$$$$

Wines to Buy:	We stick with red wines in this activity as they are the best-known and most interesting wines of Piedmont (PEED-mont). Note that while fairly common varieties, not all wine shops will carry all three bottles so you may need to hunt around a bit.
	The Dolcetto [Dul-CHET-oh] and Barbera [Bar-BEAR-ah] should be available for around $15 and a recent vintage will work perfectly well.
	For the Nebbiolo [Neb-ee-OH-lo], if on a budget look for a Langhe [LANG-eh] Nebbiolo, good examples of which can be found for around $25. Produttori del Barbareso produces a solid, widely available offering at this price point.
	If you're looking to experience Piedmont's flagship Barolo [Bar-OH-low] or Barbaresco [Bar-bar-ES-co] be prepared to spend at least $40 for an entry level bottle with a few years of aging. These two wines are made from the same grape as the Langhe Nebbiolo but come from the very best parcels of land and have additional aging requirements that elevate them to legendary status.
What to Expect:	Literally translated as "foot of the mountain", Piedmont is located in northwest Italy bordering the French and Swiss Alps and is one of most well-known and picturesque wine regions in the world. We will walk you through a tasting of Dolcetto, Barbera and Nebbiolo, the three grape varieties that dominate the region.

Piedmont Overview

Imagine sitting behind the wheel of an Alfa Romeo coupe as you wind up the hills of one of the quaint towns in Piedmont on a crisp Autumn day. Vines full of yellow and red leaves slink all the way to the side of the road, a dusting of fog bounces gently off your headlights and just in the distance you can spot one of the area's many castles sitting atop a high hill. As the fog lifts you can make out the surrounding villages, hazelnut groves and in the distance the snow-capped Alps. But enough on the scenery, let's get to the wine!

At about the same latitude as Bordeaux, the shadow effect of the Alps to the north and west brings about cold temperatures that compete with the warming effect of the Mediterranean to the south. This, combined with the fact that the region sits in a valley between mountains and hills, creates the region's nearly ever-present fog. Piedmont is a relatively cool region for grape growing and the hillsides are essential to ensuring the vines get enough sunlight. In Piedmont, it's all about location, location, location! The highest and sunniest southern-facing slopes are reserved for the prized Nebbiolo plantings that demand such prime positioning. The more adaptable Barbera and Dolcetto vines more commonly occupy the cooler sides of the hills and the valley floors.

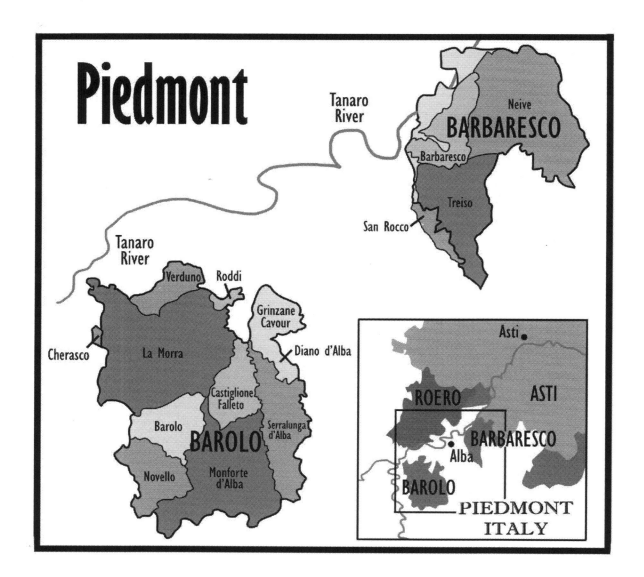

This area is widely-known for its gastronomic appeal and is the home of the coveted white truffle. Found predominately in Autumn, you may be able to find these tasty tubers at a nearby specialty Italian market where they will likely sell for $5+ per gram (about the weight of a paperclip). For a really decadent meal, shave a generous portion of truffles over buttered pasta or scrambled eggs (or use truffle oil for a lower-cost option), inhale the delicate aromas and pair with an aged Barolo.

The Wines

Pop open those bottles and let's get to drinking. If you have enough glasses, pour a glass of each for each person so you can compare and contrast as you go. If not, it's helpful to still pour at least one glass of each so you can experience the color and aroma differences before you begin drinking. Once we move to tasting we'll start with the Dolcetto, then move to the Barbera and wrap up with the Nebbiolo.

If your Nebbiolo is more than five years old, it may be worthwhile to decant the wine for an hour or so. Wine that has been bottled up for several years often needs time to breathe so that the aromas and flavors can open up. Take a sip and if your bottle initially tastes tight or sharp and the tannins cause your mouth to pucker, set it aside for at least 30 minutes and try again. Since Barberas and Dolcettos are generally consumed within a few years of bottling, those can be enjoyed immediately upon opening.

Look

Begin by looking at the three wines in front of you. As always, tilt each glass against a white surface to see more clearly. Notice how much darker the Dolcetto and Barbera are than the Nebbiolo. Based on looks alone you might guess that the Dolcetto and Barbera will be the powerhouse wines of the bunch. Hold that thought for a moment.

Describe the color of the Dolcetto. Would you say it's the darkest of the three wines, perhaps almost purple at its core?

How about the Barbera? Barberas are typically more ruby than purple, but don't be surprised if you have a Barbera that's even darker than the Dolcetto.

How about the Nebbiolo? These wines are typified by their signature brick red hue. If your Nebbiolo is a Barolo or Barbaresco look at the meniscus and notice how the brick red core of the wine gradually dissipates to clear, perhaps with brown tinges along the way. This is an indication of the wine's age and wood treatment – more time in barrels or bottle will produce a wider meniscus and introduce those orange and brown hues on the edge.

Smell

Let's now smell each of the wines, starting with the Dolcetto. Anything hit you right away?
What fruit are you smelling – more light red fruits or dark black fruits?
Any oak or vanilla aromas?
Given they are intended to be consumed while young, most Dolcettos are not aged in oak barrels so the aromas are generally more fruit forward with bright cherry and licorice dominating. Atypical for a young wine, Dolcettos can also take on plumy aromas due to the incredibly dark purple skins of the grapes.

Moving to the Barbera, how does it compare to the Dolcetto?
Are you smelling similar fruits?
Barberas are made in a wide range of styles so aromas could include lighter berries like raspberries and red cherries to darker fruits like black berries and black cherries. Barberas are also made with a wide range of oak treatment from none to a year or more, so vanilla and oak aromas may be apparent as well.

Finally let's move to the Nebbiolo. All Nebbiolos, and Barolos and Barbarescos in particular, are highly aromatic wines. How would you describe this compared to the others? This should be a clear outlier here with a more complex aroma extending to flowers (perhaps roses), herbs (maybe rosemary or sage), vegetables (we always smell tomato leaves) earth, leather, tobacco leaves and tar.

Before moving on, test yourself by closing your eyes and having your drinking partner offer you each glass to smell. Can you pick out the Nebbiolo without even looking? Once you can, remember this party trick for your next group wine tasting!

Taste

Let's now circle back around to the Dolcetto. The Dolcetto grape is a bit of a misnomer as the literal translation for the grape is "little sweet one"; however, Dolcetto is not a sweet wine. As you taste the wine, do you find that the flavor follows the aroma? Black cherry, licorice and prunes are common descriptors for Dolcetto. These wines tend to be very easy to drink given their fruit forward nature, lower acidity and soft tannins, characteristics that make them appropriate for enjoyment with or without food and inappropriate for long-term aging.

If you were to liken Dolcetto to another wine you've had before, what would you say is most similar? Many people liken it to Merlot based on its bold fruit profile and soft mouth feel – would you agree?

Let's now move on to the Barbera. With your first sip what do you notice first? Hint: it may not hit you until after you've swallowed. If you are feeling your salivary glands working overtime, it's because Barberas are naturally very high in acidity. This makes them great pairings with a wide range of typical Italian foods including pasta and pizza.

With your next sip consider more intently the taste of the wine. Common flavors range from strawberries and red cherries to black cherries, licorice and herbs. Barberas are usually aged for a period in oak barrels which can soften the acidity and add a small amount of tannins.

Their versatility has made Barbera the most planted red grape variety in Piedmont and the third most planted red in Italy after Sangiovese [San-JOE-vase-eh] and Montepulciano [MON-teh-PULL-che-AH-no]! Because Barberas come in such a wide variety of styles you may have found that your local wine merchant carried a few different bottles. For a fun side activity pick up a few and taste them side-by-side as we're doing here and find your favorite.

Finally we move on to the Nebbiolo. Look again at the wine's striking color. Based on looks alone you'd probably liken this to a Pinot Noir or other light red wine. But take a sip and prepare to be shocked.

After the Barbera the first thing you probably notice is the bracing tannin that immediately dries out your mouth. These tannins are what give Nebbiolo long aging potential. While we wouldn't recommend it for every bottle, some Barolos and Barbarescos will taste even better after 50 years!

With your second sip pay attention to the high acid that helps balance these tannins and makes Nebbiolo another great wine for food pairing.

With your third sip begin to take note of the layers of flavors. You could be tasting just about anything from a quality Nebbiolo including red cherries, oranges, truffles, mint, walnuts, coffee, leather – the list is endless.

With your fourth sip note how all of these elements – the bold flavors, the high acid, the persistent tannins – balance each other out to create a cohesive whole. This is what quality wine is all about. Barolo and Barbaresco are sometimes referred to as the king and queen of wines where Barolo is a pure powerhouse and Barbaresco has a similar but slightly softer overall profile.

Conclusion

In Italy, Barolos and Barbarescos are usually reserved for special occasions given their rich flavor and high price. Dolcetto and Barbera are more for everyday drinking. Can you see why?

In the end, what's your conclusion? Do your preferences lean towards everyday drinkers like the Dolcetto or Barbera, or do you prefer the "rip your face off" tannic structure of Nebbiolos?

As with most Italian wines, these varietals are meant to be enjoyed with food, so your preference may lie with the pairing. Try the Dolcetto with a pasta or pizza. For richer foods, like veal tartare commonly found in Piedmont, you may find that those need a higher acidity Barbera to "cut the fat." And taking a step further, you may find that a juicy steak or truffle pasta is the perfect complement for a Nebbiolo.

All For Sauvignon Blanc and Pinot Gris/Grigio

Level	◐	Bottles	🍾🍾 or 🍾🍾🍾	Price	$$$$

Wines to Buy:	You have a few options to choose from with this activity based on how many people will be joining you or how much you want to drink.
	The first option is to compare Sauvignon Blanc [SO-vin-yown BLAWNK] to either Pinot Gris [PEE-no GREE] or Pinot Grigio [PEE-no GREE-jee-oh]; the contrast will be fairly stark.
	The second option is to compare Pinot Gris to Pinot Grigio where the differences will be more subtle.
	The third option (and our favorite since it involves the most wine) is to roll this into one giant activity to compare all three!
	Whichever approach you take, look for a Sauvignon Blanc from New Zealand, a Pinot Gris from the Alsace region of northeast France, and a Pinot Grigio from either the Alto Adige region of northern Italy or from Oregon in the US. No need to spend any more than $15 on any of these bottles, but if you want to spend a little more, $30 will buy you a bottle of Cloudy Bay from New Zealand, one of the most recognized and well regarded Sauvignon Blancs in the world.
What to Expect:	Sauvignon Blanc and Pinot Gris, or Pinot Grigio as it's called in Italy, are remarkably similar in many ways: they are all high in acid, low in sugar, feature strong citrus notes and pair well with a variety of light cuisine. However, their distinguishing characteristics will put your tasting abilities to the test!

Let's start with the Sauvignon Blanc since this is the most distinctive of the bottles in front of you. If you are comparing just Pinot Gris and Pinot Grigio simply skip this section.

Sauvignon Blanc
After Airen (an unpopular grape grown predominantly in Spain and gradually being phased out for more modern varietals) and Chardonnay, Sauvignon Blanc is the most widely planted white grape in the world. Compared to the flexibility of Chardonnay, Sauvignon Blanc prefers a narrower range of climates, and cooler weather brings out its best. Areas of high heat are typically avoided as the grape will quickly become over-ripe and produce wines with dull flavors and flat acidity. While this preference for cool weather limits its growing regions and results in less variation in style (it is almost never oaked for example) it's still produced around the world in a variety of styles and flavors.

Sauvignon Blanc originated in the Bordeaux and Loire Valley regions of France, and it remains popular there to this day. Examples from the Loire Valley in particular are some of the purest, most refreshingly zesty wines in the world. The best wines from this region served as a model for early producers of the wine on the opposite side of the world in New Zealand throughout the 1970s, so much so that within a decade the tables had turned and French producers were more likely to seek inspiration from their New Zealand counterparts. For this reason we might call New Zealand the "new original" of Sauvignon Blanc. Go ahead and pour everyone a glass and let's get to tasting!

Start with your usual look, smell, taste approach and share your initial thoughts. Can everyone agree on one or two prevalent aroma and flavor descriptors?

Sauvignon Blanc's most recognizable characteristic is its piercing aroma, so focus on what you can smell as much as what you can taste. Are you picking up grassy, herbaceous notes? Think of a fresh cut lawn or a vegetable garden. These are the classic hallmark traits of any Sauvignon Blanc.

What about the overall feel of the wine? Is this big and bold or light and airy? Wine experts will often describe Sauvignon Blanc as crisp, elegant and fresh, even relative to other white wines. Do you agree, or do you find some weight to your wine?

Beyond these general characteristics your wine will vary based on its origin, with flavors ranging from aggressively grassy in cooler regions to sweetly tropical in warmer locales. Sauvignon Blanc from cooler climates tends to be more acidic with green fruit flavors such as zesty citrus and green apple, and herbaceous flavors of grass and bell pepper accompanied by mild tropical fruit and stone fruit. In warmer climates the wine tends towards a rounder, flowery, tropical fruit character with more muted grassy notes. Have another sip and decide if your wine is closer to a lime or a peach. Does the flavor that you find align with your expectation based on the climate of its origin?

Assuming you've selected a New Zealand Sauvignon Blanc for this activity, you should find the aromatic and flavor profile dominated by a strong grapefruit character. This flavor profile tends to be consistent across producers from the region. Do you pick up any of this in your wine?

This is the style that introduced New Zealand wine to the world: intensely perfumed, more obviously fruity than the Loire Valley prototype, with just a hint of grass and sweetness. New Zealand's widely varied terrain can create a diversity of flavors from vineyards across multiple sites with different soil types and micro-climates. Winemakers can blend early-ripening grapes from the valleys and their grassy, herbaceous notes with late-ripening grapes from the hillsides and their lush tropical flavors to create a balanced, complex wine with layers of nuance. The generally cool climate of the area allows for a long growing season that further distinguishes New Zealand Sauvignon Blanc's fully ripe grapes with naturally balanced sugar and acid.

What do you think about the aging potential of your wine? Odds are your wine is from a recent vintage because Sauvignon Blanc from almost all regions of the world is usually consumed young. The wine usually does not benefit from aging as its grassy notes devolve into overly-vegetal notes of asparagus and peas. Dry and sweet Sauvignon Blanc from Bordeaux and the Loire Valley are some of the few examples with aging potential. In the case of Bordeaux, Sauvignon Blanc is a key component, along with Sémillon [Sem-ee-OWN] and Muscadelle [Moos-kah-DELL], in the sweet wines of Sauternes and Barsac that can age for decades, taking on a toasted honey character as the wine turns from bright yellow to burnt amber over the years.

You may have seen the term Fumé Blanc [Foo-MAY blawnk] on a bottle of wine before and assumed this was the grape varietal. In fact, Fumé Blanc is nothing more than regular old Sauvignon Blanc. Robert Mondavi invented the term Fumé Blanc in the late 1960s when he was having difficulties selling wine under the then-unpopular label of Sauvignon Blanc. So like any good marketer, he rebranded! The "Fumé" part of the name literally translates to "smoke", but this has nothing to do with the flavor of the wine, rather it is derived from Pouilly-Fumé, one of the premier regions for French Sauvignon Blanc made in a dry style. Mondavi chose not to trademark the term and it's now widely used to indicate a dry, new world style Sauvignon Blanc.

Pinot Gris / Pinot Grigio

Let's move now to the Pinot Gris and Pinot Grigio. Much like Syrah and Shiraz, while Pinot Grigio and Pinot Gris are the same grape the two names have come to infer two different styles of wine. If you are only using Pinot Gris in this activity to compare against Sauvignon Blanc you can skip to that section. Otherwise get started by pouring everyone a glass of Pinot Grigio.

Pinot Grigio

Odds are you've had Pinot Grigio before whether you realized it or not. Order a generic white wine at any bar or restaurant and its likely Pinot Grigio in the glass. It is almost universally inoffensive with few distinguishing characteristics that merit praise or complaint. Go ahead and enjoy a few sips. We challenge you to identify any major aroma or flavor character beyond crisp citrus notes and bright acidity. Anything stand out for you? While French in origin, it's really the Italians who popularized the grape through expressions such as this that are typically light-bodied and crisp with floral aromas and fresh citrus and occasionally stone fruit flavors.

What do you think about this wine's aging potential? Would you expect further complexity to emerge over time? Unlikely. Easy-drinking and intended for early consumption, these wines are not meant to push boundaries or challenge palates. Cellaring for a few years would likely do more harm than good, muting the vibrant fruit and acidity without revealing any lurking character.

Because of its immense popularity, Pinot Grigio is mass produced and sub-$10 magnums are ubiquitous in grocery stores and the lower end section of wine shops. These bottles are invariably one-dimensional, bright, zippy, floral and citrus dominated wines. But this doesn't mean that quality versions of Pinot Grigio don't exist. Northern Italy produces more interesting expressions that are complex and structured. Wine from the Alto Adige region of northern Italy in particular is noted for its purity and intensity and depth of flavor. If you were able to find one of these bottles for this activity, in what ways does it stand above the more generic Pinot Grigios we've discussed so far?

Pinot Gris

Let's move on to the Pinot Gris. Go ahead and pour everyone a glass alongside the Pinot Grigio if possible, otherwise you can reuse the same glasses. These wines will be similar enough you don't even need to rinse in between. Have a few sips. Any differences immediately apparent? In contrast to Pinot Grigio, Pinot Gris tends to be made in a slightly rounder, broader, richer profile. Initially you may feel this as much as you taste it. This is a slightly weightier wine with a more viscous texture.

In terms of flavors, Pinot Gris from the Alsace region of northeastern France (in additional to quality versions available from Oregon and New Zealand) is notably fuller-bodied and richer than its Italian counterpart. Notice how the wine coats your mouth more so than the Pinot Grigio. Still an easy drinker, even without food, but there's a little more substance to this wine.

Compared to Pinot Grigio, it also tends to have greater potential for aging. What additional aromas and flavors would you expect to emerge from your wine after a few years? Likely a darkening of the wine, along with some deeper stone fruit flavors corresponding with more muted citrus notes. Mild baking spice notes such as cloves and nutmeg may also emerge from quality bottlings.

Compared to Sauvignon Blanc
Either of these wines will likely seem a little dull to you in comparison to the Sauvignon Blanc. They lack the grassy, vegetal notes and typically don't offer as intense floral or tropical aromas. But this isn't necessarily a bad thing. Sometimes a milder, less-distinctive, less-assertive wine has its place.

Conclusion
Before we finish with these wines, consider what foods you might pair with each. White wines are generally best with lighter fare of course, but you've tasted two or three marginally different styles here that you may find lend themselves to a particular time and place as much as cuisine.

Sauvignon Blanc pairs well with stinky cheese and fish, and is one of the few wines that work well with sushi. Its herbal notes also enable it to pair well with greens so can be a great accompaniment to salads or other dishes with prominent leafy flavors such as basil, rosemary and cilantro.

Quality Pinot Gris has a full, round taste similar to a light Chardonnay and can pair well with medium rich dishes and even some lighter sauces. By comparison, Pinot Grigio is a natural "porch pounder" or picnic wine. It's crisp and light and perfect for a hot day when you just want a drink without thinking too much about it. In terms of food pairing, this might work well with vegetable or light seafood appetizers. Food isn't necessary though and it would also pair well with more Pinot Grigio!

So in the end what did you prefer? The assertiveness of the Sauvignon Blanc, or the mellowness of the Pinot Gris and Pinot Grigio?
Did you like the more rounded profile of the Pinot Gris, or did the directness of the Pinot Grigio match your palate?
Or did you miss an oaky element that would be more prevalent in other white wines such as Chardonnay? Serious wine drinkers tend more towards Pinot Gris than Pinot Grigio, and more toward Sauvignon Blanc than either. But it's all about finding what appeals to you, and matching your wine with a suitable time and place. Even those much maligned $10 magnums of Pinot Grigio could hit the spot at a boozy beach BBQ with friends!

All For Chardonnay

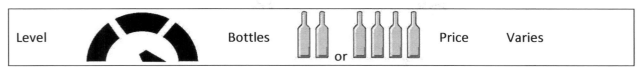

Level		Bottles		Price	Varies

Wines to Buy:	As with the previous activity, you have a few options about how to tackle this one. We say four bottles is always better than two, but if only selecting two bottles go with an unoaked cool climate wine, such as a Chablis [Sha-BLEE], and an oaked warm climate counterpoint, such as a California Chardonnay. Good examples of each should be available for under $20 from old world regions and closer to $10 for new world regions. If you're going with four bottles, also add an oaked Chardonnay from a cooler region such as a New Zealand and an unoaked Chardonnay from Southern Italy. Reference the table below for other options.
What to Expect:	Chardonnay is a remarkable grape, capable of being grown in almost any wine region of the world and a vast array of styles. In this activity we explore oaked vs. unoaked and cool vs. warm climate Chardonnay. You will learn how climate and winemaking technique influences the wine, develop an ability to pick out tell-tale elements of its production and understand the elements you prefer to inform your future enjoyment.

Few grapes are as versatile as Chardonnay and the bottles you've selected will offer a clear contrast highlighting the differences in climate and production that result in radically different wines. Go ahead and open all the bottles. We're going to work our way through the grid below starting in the top left, so start by pouring everyone a glass of the cool climate unoaked wine. If only using two bottles for this activity then simply skip to those that you have.

		Wood Treatment	
		Unoaked	**Oaked**
Climate	**Cool**	Chablis (central France) Germany	Walker Bay (coastal South Africa) Marlborough (New Zealand) Casablanca Valley, Central Valley (Chile) Finger Lakes New York (USA) Argentinean Andes
	Warm	Mâconnais (central France) Southern Italy	Sonoma California, Los Carneros California (USA) Languedoc (southern France) Argentinean desert Yarra Valley, Adelaide Hills (southeastern Australia)

Unoaked & cool (…as a cucumber – which you may get hints of in the wine)

Chablis is a good choice for this type of wine as it is the standard bearer for unoaked Chardonnay and it's affordable and readily available (although a German Chardonnay would work just as well). Chablis is from the Chablis region of Burgundy in north-central France. Look, smell and taste the wine so you gain a quick impression of what it's all about. In a word, Chablis can often be described as "clean." It's the purest expression of the Chardonnay grape produced with minimal manipulation. Marvel at its simplicity….

Chablis lies on the same latitude as the state of Maine, and its relatively cool climate produces a grape that is naturally high in acid. After your next sip pay attention to your salivary glands to see how long they remain active. Lean forward, look down with your nose pointed to the ground and notice your salivary glands. Do you feel a mouth-watering sensation? Now take another sip and concentrate on the flavors you experience.

No doubt you taste lemon as is common for a high acid wine. Looking beyond citrus flavors, if the wine were an apple, would it be green, yellow or red? High acidity Chablis is often reminiscent of green apple and green pear.

Have another sip and see if you can find any flavors behind the dominant fruit character, perhaps lurking vegetal flavors of cucumber or lettuce? Taste closely. Such subtle flavors are only possible because the underlying purity of the grapes has not been overlaid with oak. Chablis is fermented in stainless steel tanks that preserve a clean, crisp, fresh, almost flinty taste. Unoaked production works well with these wines so their natural freshness is highlighted without being brought down by some of the heavier flavors of toast and vanilla that we'll experience in a moment.

Oaked & cool
Let's now move to the wine in the top right of the grid produced in a similarly cool climate but with the introduction of oak. We've provided a few examples of this type of wine, but you have so many options you can't go wrong. Go ahead and have a sip or three.

Notice that the acidity is still there, though perhaps you aren't feeling it quite as much as with your first wine. But ask yourself the same question about what color apple this tastes like, and you probably get the same answer as the cool climate produces a similar fruit profile.

The more prominent difference is the influence of the wood treatment that will lend flavors of toast, vanilla, cloves, nutmeg or baking spice. These flavors likely aren't overpowering as these are still relatively delicate expressions of Chardonnay thanks to the cool climate. But with these two glasses you get a very clear idea of the difference between oaked and unoaked wine of any variety.

Unoaked & warm
Working our way to the bottom left of the grid we're stepping away from the oak for a moment and into warmer territory. Before you have a sip of this one, revisit your first wine to remind yourself of its bracing acidity and green fruit character. Now contrast this with your first sip of the warmer climate wine.

You probably notice the lower acidity immediately. In comparison you may find this wine tastes smoother, more muted, almost a little flat. These aren't bad qualities, they just highlight the difference. After a few more sips your palate will adapt and you'll be able to pick out some of the finer elements.

Like your first bottle, this is still a very pure expression of the same Chardonnay grape, but the warmer climate produces a remarkably different wine. You should find that the citrus and green fruit character has been replaced with more tropical fruit flavors. With your next sip look for traces of bananas, pineapples and mangoes.

You may find your wine has more of a melon or stone fruit character with hints of peaches or nectarines. If you enjoyed a Chablis as your first bottle, Mâconnais [MAK-oh-nay] makes a nice choice for this bottle as it is located just a 2-hour drive south into the southern-most, warmest area of Burgundy.

Oaked & warm

This brings us to our final bottle for this activity in the lower right of the grid. Before even taking your first sip of this wine, compare its color to the previous wines. You likely see that it's noticeably darker with golden or faint brown tinges that indicate it has spent significant time in contact with oak. Give it a few swirls and smell the wine.

Powerful, right? Are you smelling similar aromas to the cool-climate oaked bottle you tasted first? The profile of this wine is likely even stronger, and you may be able to find some element of butter. This is because winemakers seeking a weighty style Chardonnay will take it through an extra step called "malolactic fermentation." This is a process that converts the malic acid present in all grapes into lactic acid. The result is softer tannins and added dairy notes like butter and cream to the aroma and taste of the wine. Consider the different tanginess between a green apple and yogurt. The bright, effervescent green apple tanginess is malic acid. The creamy, smooth yogurt tanginess is lactic acid. If you've ever had a wine that smelled like buttery movie theater popcorn, including perhaps the wine in front of you now, this is why.

Take another sip and note the feel of the wine in your mouth. Swish it around a little. We're far removed from the clean, crisp, pure wine we started with! What flavors are you getting?

Given the warmer climate for this wine, you may get more intensely tropical fruits including bananas and pineapples. You might also detect some yeasty or bready flavors that are a result of the winemaking process. Remarkable that these are the same Chardonnay grapes we've been drinking all along, but now with a warm climate and oak treatment that create an entirely different experience!

Because it's relatively easy to grow and can be heavily manipulated during and after fermentation, there are extreme styles of Chardonnay that turn off some consumers. Many California producers of Chardonnay in particular have taken a heavy handed approach to production that results in wines with strong oak and butter flavors. There's nothing necessarily wrong with this, and some people love these wines, but they are on the far end of the flavor spectrum, and therefore a turnoff to many. Some of this bad reputation is overblown. In fact, many producers of California Chardonnay have recognized the criticism and evolving consumer taste and have started to dial it back. But mentioning "California Chard" to a serious wine drinker may elicit eye-rolls and groans of over-oaked butter bombs. Although it's much maligned, it does make sense that winemakers would opt to produce such a product. Warm weather flavors should naturally work well with malolactic fermentation and oak manipulation. Think buttered rum, bananas foster, pineapple upside-down cake or peach pie. These are great flavors! But for many it's not what they look for in their wine. What do you think?

Conclusion

Now that you've tried them all, which wine did you prefer? Do you like the purity of the unoaked cool climate Chard, the oaked warm climate opposite, or something in between?

For us, it's simply a matter of pairing the ideal wine with the time, place and meal at hand. Unoaked cool climate Chards are great on a warm day with light fish or poultry dishes. Oaked warm climate Chards are better when the weather is warmer and you have a heartier meal (or will be drinking without food and want a substantial wine!) If you tend to prefer white wines to red, oaked warm weather Chardonnay is also a great accompaniment to many foods traditionally paired with red wine, and it serves as a great transition wine from heavy whites to lighter reds.

All For Riesling

Level		Bottles		Price	

Wines to Buy:	Although Riesling [REE-sling] is produced in several areas of the world, including some in the US, we recommend you find a wine from Germany for this activity since it is their hallmark grape. German Riesling is helpfully categorized by sugar level, so head out to your local wine merchant to seek out an off-dry "Spätlese" [SPET-less-a] or "Auslese" [AUS-lessa] that you chill thoroughly. If unable to find a German wine for this activity, look for the popular Chateau Ste. Michelle line from Washington State. They offer a complement of Rieslings at each sweetness level at a low price point.
What to Expect:	Widely available in an easy-drinking style with residual sweetness that masks its alcohol, Riesling is a gateway wine for many new drinkers. But it's much more than a simple sipper; for many connoisseurs it's the world's greatest white wine varietal. In this activity you'll pair an off-dry (meaning slightly sweet) Riesling with spicy food that will help you appreciate its complexity and opportunities for revealing food pairings. This is a great activity to pair with spicy Asian cuisine such as Chinese (especially Szechuan) or Thai takeout. Barring that, any dish with decent spice and heat will do.

Time to eat! Plate your meal, pop and pour that Riesling and let's get started! Before you chow down, start by enjoying the wine on its own by noting the aromas and initial tastes you experience. With any off-dry wine keep an eye out (a tongue out?) for the residual sweetness after you swallow. It's this hint of sugar at the end that distinguishes this from a dry (little or no sweetness) or sweet wine (which would start sweet and remain sweet throughout).

Riesling is always grown in relatively cool climates since a warmer climate would burn off the delicate aromatics it's capable of achieving. This is why Germany and Austria are most famous for their aromatic white wines rather than their reds. A byproduct of the cooler climate is a grape that develops naturally higher acidity which in turn allows for the wine to be produced with higher sugar levels while remaining balanced. Think of acid and sugar on opposing sides of a seesaw: you can maintain a quality wine with more of one (sugar), as long as you have more of the other (acid). With your next sip pay particular attention to this acidity. Note how you salivate on the wine's attack. The sugar then comes in just at the end to wipe this away and leave you with a mildly sweet note on the finish.

Now that you have the sugar and the acid down let's look for the aromas and flavors. Most Riesling is fruity and floral rather than herbaceous, like Sauvignon Blanc, or oaky and buttery like Chardonnay. But depending on the climate in which it's grown, it can take on a variety of characteristics. Riesling from a cooler climate will have notes of green apples, flowers and citrus (especially lemon and lime). Riesling from a more moderate climate will have correspondingly warmer, mellower notes of yellow apples, stone fruit (peaches, nectarines, apricots) and tropical fruit (pineapple and mango). Can you tell what you have?

After you've made a guess see if you can find any notes on the bottle detailing its origin and check the map to see if you were right. Mosel is Germany's most famous region for Riesling, and due to its northerly location wines from there tend to be lighter with crisp acidity, floral characteristics and bright citrus rather than tropical fruit flavors. The warmer Mittelrhein and Rheingau regions near Mosel, and Pfalz and Baden regions further south, are more likely to produce dry Rieslings with rounder stone fruit and tropical flavors with mellower acidity.

After your next sip while the touch of sweetness remains on your palate take a bite of spicy food. Notice how the extreme contrast of sweet to spicy accentuates the food's heat. After you've swallowed another bite, take a sip of wine. Note how the acid washes away the spicy flavor and the sweetness is now accentuated. You may even taste bright, sweet flavors you didn't detect before the food. What's happening here is one extreme, either the fruit in the wine or the spice in the food, is highlighting the opposite flavor in the pairing. In the same way that a sunny day seems brighter when you first open your blinds in the morning, a sweet wine tastes even sweeter when paired with spicy food.

While you enjoy the rest of your meal, consider if you like the wine better with the food or on its own. A fuller-flavored Riesling with bold tropical fruits and higher sweetness may be more appealing with a meal that compliments its intensity. Equally, a more subdued Riesling may be better on its own or with a milder meal. Sushi is a popular pairing with dry Riesling.

Riesling can be made in a variety of styles, it's not just sweet wine. The easiest way to determine the sweetness level is to look for the terms "Trocken" (dry) or "Halbtrocken" (off-dry) on the label. Beyond that and you'll need to understand a few details of the German labeling system we've summarized in the table below. Labeling hierarchy is based on the ripeness of the grapes when harvested, which typically translates into the sweetness level of the resulting wine. Ripeness, quality and price are highly correlated in Rieslings, in ascending order:

Category	Tasting notes	Food pairing
Kabinett	Light body, dry to off-dry, high acid, green fruits (green apples), low alcohol (usually 8-10%).	Sushi
Spätlese	Translates to "late picked." Medium-body, can be made dry, off-dry or sweet, with intense flavors of citrus (lemon) and tropical fruit (pineapple).	Spicy dishes
Auslese	Translates to "picked out", indicating the grapes bunches are selected for their ripeness. Fuller body, off-dry or sweet, more intense tropical fruit (pineapple, mango).	Spicy or sweet dishes
Beerenauslese	Translates to "berries picked out", indicating not just entire bunches but individual grapes were selected for extreme ripeness.	Fruit-based dessert or blue cheese.
Trockenbeerenauslese	Translates to "dried berries picked out", indicating berries already selected for their sweetness were then dried to be more like sweet raisins before being fermented. Sweet wine, highly viscous, almost honey-like.	Drink after or in place of a dessert
Eiswein	One of the sweetest wines produced in the world, made from frozen grapes that removes much of the water from the wine-making process, resulting in a highly concentrated, syrupy wine.	Drink after or in place of a dessert

 Though most commonly consumed while still young, quality Riesling is age-worthy due to its intensity and variety of flavors that will evolve over time. Older Riesling can take on particularly unique qualities of smoke and gasoline (yes, gasoline!) along with honey and toast.

All For Pinot Noir

Level		Bottles		Price	$$$$

Wines to Buy:	The world's best Pinot Noir comes from the Burgundy [BUR-gun-dee] region of central France (the same region as Champagne) with the top producers commanding prices in the thousands of dollars per bottle. Google "DRC wine price" to laugh (or cry) at what a bottle of Domaine de la Romanee-Conti will run you these days. Not to worry, you'll do plenty fine for this activity with a bottle in the $20-30 range. Speak with your local wine merchant for a recommendation and venture outside of Burgundy for your bottle only if you must as Pinot Noir is more sensitive to its terroir than many other grapes. Your second bottle should come from the Willamette [Will-AM-it] Valley in northwest Oregon where quality bottles can be found for $20. As with the first bottle, stick to the Willamette Valley if possible as our notes below are specifically geared toward wine from the region.
What to Expect:	Pinot Noir is a notoriously difficult grape to grow. Its thin skins make it the Goldilocks of grapes. If the weather is too cold it will not develop its trademark light fruit flavors and instead take on excessive vegetal notes (think cabbage and wet leaves). If too hot, it will get sunburned and become overly jammy and lose any sense of delicacy. Consequently most quality Pinot Noir is grown in just a few select regions of the world. In this activity you will compare wines from two such regions: Burgundy, the standard against which all Pinot Noir is judged, and the Willamette Valley, an emerging region of Oregon producing wines that rival its French counterpart.

Look

The delicacy of the wines in this activity make it especially important to be able to experience both simultaneously, so start by pouring everyone a glass of each wine. Hold the two glasses in front of you against a white background. How would you describe the color of the wines? Yes, they are red, but what hue of red? Do they lean towards the darker red or maroon and purple end of the spectrum, or are they lighter, almost pink on the edges?

 Note the correct pronunciation of "Willamette" unexpectedly places the emphasis on the second syllable and rhymes with "damn it."

 Pinot Noir is known by many names: in Italy it is called (somewhat obviously) Pinot Nero, in Germany it is called (somewhat less obviously) Spätburgunder. Though a mouthful, in fact the German term for the grape is very descriptive: "Spät" means "Late" referring to the grapes' ideal harvest time late in the season, and "Burgunder" means "Burgundy" referring to the region where the grapes originated.

Unless you have a Pinot Noir from an extremely warm climate like Australia or southern California, most likely your wines are lightly colored and nearly transparent on the meniscus. What does this tell you about the flavor profile you should expect? A lighter red wine such as this will more likely have aromas and flavors of bright red fruits such as strawberries and cranberries than dark red fruits like plums and black cherries. Keep this in mind when we smell and taste in a moment.

Look at the wines against a white background again. Regardless of hue, note their intensity and how exceptionally light they are, even at their core. Hold one of the glasses in front of this page and notice you can actually read through the wine! All grape juice, even from red grapes, is white. Red wines get their color from contact with the grape skins. Pinot Noirs are typically so light in color because their skins are so thin, an attribute that contributes to difficulty in growing and harvesting them and thus their high price. Grape skins are also the primary source of a wine's tannins. So putting two and two together, with such a light colored wine you should expect light tannins. We'll find out if that holds true in a moment.

Smell
Next, swirl and sniff your Burgundy. Take your time before sharing your experience with your drinking partners. Try to pick out at least three distinct aromas before anyone says anything. Once everyone has had a moment, take turns sharing what you've smelled so far. After each descriptor smell again to see if you can find it. This is where wine tasting in a group gets really fun as people will find smells and flavors that you didn't on the first try, but afterwards can't understand how you missed it!

Based on the color of the wine, what would you expect to smell? We've already mentioned light red fruits like strawberries and cranberries. Do you smell any other fruits? Red cherries perhaps?
What about earthy aromas like mushrooms, wet leaves and manure?
Or more obviously pleasing floral aromas such as roses and violets?
Burgundies are made in a variety of styles, but typical hallmarks are red fruits, violets and forest floor aromas such as truffles and damp earth. Depending on the wood treatment you may also find whiffs of toast and smoke.

Move on to your Willamette Pinot now and repeat the process. How do these aromas differ from the Burgundy? Is this what you would expect based on any variation in the color? Compared to Burgundies, and old world wines in general, Willamette Pinot Noir and new world wines tend to me more fruit-forward without prevalent manure and earthy aromas. So here you may find the red fruits are more dominant, though still with a noticeable presence of mushrooms or herbs.

Continue to go back and forth between the two wines, seeing if their contrast helps to highlight any additional aromas. Are you already starting to develop a preference between the two?

Taste
Finally! We hope you've been able to hold out until now as following the steps above will have prepared you to fully appreciate your wines' complexities. Go ahead and enjoy, starting with the Burgundy. Don't worry so much about analyzing the wine with your first few sips, just kick back and drink. After several sips your mouth will have adjusted to the wine's acidity and we can start to walk through some of its attributes.

First off, does the wine taste the way it smells or are you surprised by anything?
Do those earthy aromas translate to the taste?
Are you finding the same red fruits you smelled earlier or picking up anything different now?
If you taste something new, go back to swirling and smelling to see if you can find that aroma. Some common Pinot Noir flavors you may pick up more so than their aromas include mint and cinnamon, especially on the finish.

Let's try the Willamette Valley now. Again, do you find that the flavors match the aromas?
How does this wine taste compared to the Burgundy?

You'll likely find it to be more intense and fruit-forward with earthy and herbal flavors playing a more muted role. These wines are often fairly tart, so you may taste cranberries and fresh strawberries more distinctly. After you've enjoyed this wine for a bit go back to the Burgundy and see if you detect anything new.

With the flavors covered, let's focus on the tannins. Note how lightly tannic both wines are. Just what we expected based on their color. Consider how these minimal tannins are balanced by the wine's fresh acidity and red fruits to create a harmonious experience. With your next sip pay attention to how either wine feels in your mouth. High end Pinot Noir is rich, but still light and nimble with substantial flavor despite its delicacy. These wines are prized for their silky smooth texture, typically with just enough tannin to keep things interesting and contribute to a lasting finish.

Conclusion

Before discussing which of these two bottles you preferred, what did you think of Pinot Noir in general?

What stood out compared to other wines you've enjoyed?

Did you like the relatively light red fruits and earthy flavors, or would you have preferred a darker, juicier wine?

How about the tannins? Did you find the wine had a smooth, silky texture, and if so, would you have preferred more grip from fuller tannins?

Finally, what about the cost? Were these wines a good value for you taste preferences?

Check out the **Boozy Movie Night** activity earlier in this book to catch up on the modern classic wine movie Sideways that sparked renewed interest in West Coast Pinot Noir, infamously at the expense of Merlot.

Quality Pinot Noir is typically fairly expensive ($20+). Consequently many winemakers want to produce Pinot Noir so they can charge high prices as well. But with Pinot Noir it's hard to find a bargain. If you see Pinot for less than $10, examine the label and see if you can deduce why it's unlikely to be worth even that. Is it from a region ill-suited to the grape's needs (for example, is it from a warm weather climate and thus likely to be jammy)?

Pinot Noir carries an air of myth and mystery about it which can be fun, but can also lead to the perception of inflated prices for a return that can't be easily quantified. If you didn't enjoy these bottles, or liked them well enough but thought they were too expensive, don't worry. Give Pinot Noir a break while you focus on appreciating other wines and come back to it again in a year to see if your thoughts have changed. It's not many drinkers' first favorite wine, but is often a rediscovered favorite by more experienced connoisseurs.

All For Cabernet Sauvignon & Merlot

Level		Bottles		Price	

Wines to Buy:	You'll need two bottles of red Bordeaux: a "right bank" bottle dominated by Merlot, and a "left bank" bottle dominated by Cabernet Sauvignon. If you're unfamiliar with these terms we will explain more fully in this activity, until then trust the advice of your local merchant. While the finest bottles from the region routinely sell for hundreds or even thousands of dollars, there are plenty of quality offerings from as little as $10. We recommend bottles in the $15-20 range. Bordeaux is notorious for its variation across vintages, so ideally you'll be able to find two wines from the same year. 2009 and 2010 were two recent high-quality vintages; if those aren't available then 2015 is a good bet. Otherwise feel free to mix vintages – the hallmark attributes of each grape will still be apparent.
What to Expect:	Cabernet Sauvignon (which we'll refer to simply as "Cab" for the rest of this activity) and Merlot are almost always blended to some degree. It's rare to find a wine that is truly 100% of either, despite what the bottle may be telling you. But even in a blend, one of the two grapes will typically dominate. We'll use a comparison of two bottles produced from opposite sides of the river that defines the Bordeaux region to illustrate the differences.

Think of Cab vs. Merlot as a virtual tour through the famous wine growing region of Bordeaux, France. The two banks of the Gironde River that separates the region are home to what are widely considered the world's finest examples of Cab (characteristic of "left bank" Bordeaux) and Merlot (characteristic of "right bank" Bordeaux). Why do the two banks of the river produce such different wines? It all comes down to soil. The soil of the right bank is mostly clay and sand that retain moisture. Merlot thrives in a water-rich environment, drinking up the water and producing rich, plump grapes full of red berry flavors. The soil of the left bank on the other hand is predominantly gravel and stone that drain water away from the vines. This is preferable for the Cab grapes that need to be stressed and starved of water in order to produce dense grapes with rich blackberry and spice flavors.

If you have enough stemware, pour everyone a glass of each wine so you can experience both side-by-side. If you don't have enough, start with the Cab first.

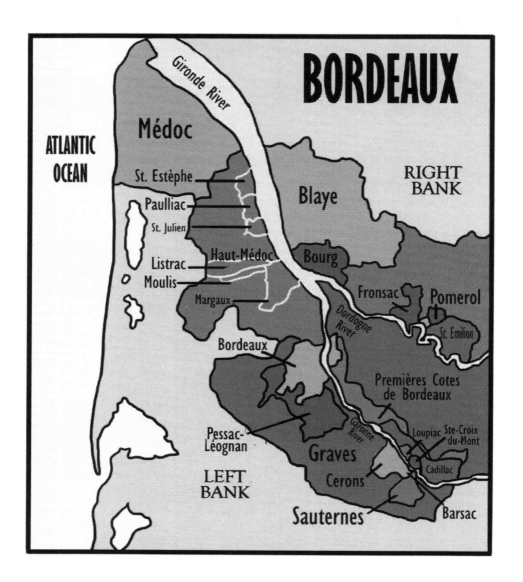

Look

The appearance of the two wines is likely very similar, and both should look like darker, fuller-bodied wines. You may find the Cab is slightly darker than the Merlot, but both wines are a blend of up to five grape varieties legally allowed in Bordeaux, so there won't be much difference.

Only five grape varietals are allowed in red wine from Bordeaux: Cabernet Sauvignon, Cabernet Franc, Merlot, Malbec, Petit Verdot [Pe-TEE ver-DOUGH] and Carménère [Car-men-YAIR]. Cab and Merlot are the stars with each of the other three grapes, with the occasional exception of Cab Franc, rarely contributing more than 10% to the blend. Malbec is more famously used in the Cahors region of southwest France and the Mendoza region of Argentina. Petit Verdot is primarily a blending grape rarely bottled as a single varietal wine. Carménère originated in France but is now rarely seen in the country, instead finding suitable growing sites and newfound popularity in Chile.

Smell

Let's start by enjoying the aroma of the Cab. First, look past the fruit aromas and focus on the impact of the wood treatment on the wine. Classic Bordeaux is said to have a "cigar box" aroma of wood, leaves and smoke. This comes from its time spent aging in oak barrels, typically for 1-2 years, before bottling. Now let's circle back and focus on the fruit. While a seasoned nose may be able to pick out the other grapes in the blend, we'll focus solely on the Cab grape that no doubt dominates. Given the description of the left bank's soil that produces rich blackberry and spice notes, first look for these elements. What do you find? You may smell blackberry, dark cherry, spice, licorice, possibly even coffee notes.
Does one of these dominate?
How does this complement the earlier aromas of wood and smoke?

Let's now move to the Merlot. You may find the same cigar box aroma, but if you do it's likely somewhat muted compared to the Cab. If you're now thinking that the fruit characteristics would also have to be different to keep the wine in balance, you'd be right! Given the possibly lighter appearance of the wine compared to the Cab, you would expect to find lighter fruit characteristics. Look for red cherry, plum and blueberry notes. The vanilla from the wood treatment may also be more apparent than with the Cab.

Taste

Finally we get to the heart of the matter! Let's taste these delicious wines.

The flavors of Cab and Merlot from Bordeaux are highly influenced by their age. Younger wines will be more concentrated and fruit forward than older wines, which take on a softer and more integrated character. This doesn't mean flavors disappear as the wines age, rather it means the edges are softened – the highs are mellowed, allowing you to taste some of the subtler flavors that were always lurking beneath. Keep the age of your wines in mind as you continue.

Starting with the Cab, take a few sips and consider first the fruit characteristics. Do they follow the nose of blackberry and dark cherry?
What about other flavors of spice, chocolate, licorice or coffee?
How specific can you get with any of these descriptors?
If you taste spices, is it of the green or black pepper variety, or more like cloves and anise?
If coffee, is it dark roasted coffee or espresso, or something lighter like a French vanilla.

Consider next the tannins of the wine. Would you rate this as a highly tannic wine? Most Cabs produce a drying sensation in the mouth and are considered very tannic, especially in their youth. These tannins, often described as chunky or blocky in young wines, pair with the strong fruit and wood flavors to create a balanced whole. In time, these tannins will soften and mellow along with the fruit flavors to maintain that consistent balance. It's rare and disappointing to find a Cab that lacks sufficient tannin to support its powerful fruit and wood character.

Finally, consider the finish of the Cab. Note how the tannins allow the flavors to persist long after you've finished a sip. Do you like this feeling and taste, or do you prefer a "cleaner" wine that is gone the moment you swallow? A long finish is typically prized because it enhances the wine's accompaniment to a meal. It's hard to both eat and drink at the exact same moment, so having a wine with a long finish allows you to take a sip, swallow, and then enjoy a bite of food that combines with the lingering taste enabled by the tannins.

Moving next to the Merlot, how does the taste compare?

Do you pick up the taste of red cherries, plums and blueberries that you smelled earlier?

Again, what about spices? Do these taste more muted compared to the Cab?

How do the tannins compare? Are they less prevalent? It would make sense if so. Given the softer fruit character of Merlot, winemakers will typically be more cautious with their wood treatment and aim for a wine with more mellow tannins to balance with the subtler taste. How does the finish compare to the Cab? With softer tannins you shouldn't necessarily expect a shorter finish as talented winemakers will aim for a persistent finish regardless of the levels of fruit and tannin.

Merlot was once one of the most popular wines in the world, but that changed when the 2004 hit movie *Sideways* expressed a dissenting view. In the film's most enduring scene, Paul Giamatti's cantankerous Pinot Noir-loving character Miles trashes the varietal: "If anyone orders Merlot, I'm leaving! I am not drinking any f***ing Merlot!" Check out the **Boozy Movie Night** activity earlier in this book to watch for yourself!

Soon after the release of the film the reputation of Merlot tanked. In California alone growers pulled out more than 10,000 acres of Merlot vines. But at its core the wine's downfall was due to a lot more than Miles's *Sideways* rant. Many California vintners' knee-jerk response to the wine's popularity in the 1990s was to plant more, which resulted in vines growing in places with unsuitable soil and climate. With the wine's popularity waning starting in the mid 2000's, many of these ill-considered plantings were uprooted as Merlot production fell. Since then the pendulum has started swinging back and Merlot is seeing a resurgence in its popularity. And rightfully so. When made with care it can be delicious, with a silky, red cherry character and mouth-watering roundness that give it an immediate appeal.

Conclusion

It's incredible to think that these two very different wines were produced from the same five grape varieties mere miles apart from each other. In fact, both of your bottles likely state on the label in red capital letters "MIS EN BOUTEILLE AU CHATEAU" which means the wine was produced on site. The Cab and Merlot grapes in your glass were grown just across the river from each other. The wines were then fermented and aged at on-site facilities, and finally bottled and packaged for shipping from their respective sides of the river. Simply put, the first time the grapes in your wine were more than a few miles apart was when the finished bottles shipped out of France for you to purchase.

So far we've been highly complimentary to both of these wines, and you can probably sense we are big fans of Bordeaux. But before we wrap up, let's play a game. If you had to describe one of these wines as "a punch in the face" and the other as "fat and flabby", neither of which we'd consider terms of endearment, which would you apply to the Cab and which would you apply to the Merlot? At their worst, Cabs can be overpowering and unpleasant. With too much water they become sweet and cloying, and with too much sun they over-ripen, produce too much alcohol on fermentation, and simply get too powerful. Plenty of people like a hearty wine, but nobody likes to be punched in the face. With Merlot, too little water produces a thin, astringent character and a lack of control from the winemaker results in a flat, flabby wine with little structure or character. There's nothing wrong with a mellow wine, but flat and boring is never a pleasure.

So in the end what did you prefer? Do you like the intensity and ruggedness of the Cab or the brighter, red fruit character of the Merlot?

Were either of these wines lacking elements you would have preferred?

If looking for new world examples of Cab and Merlot, you can't do much better than the west coast of the US. Look for a Cabernet Sauvignon from California (in particular, Napa and Sonoma) or a Merlot from Washington State (in particular Walla Walla, Red Mountain or Columbia Valley.)

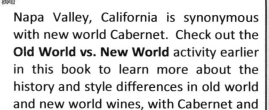 Napa Valley, California is synonymous with new world Cabernet. Check out the **Old World vs. New World** activity earlier in this book to learn more about the history and style differences in old world and new world wines, with Cabernet and Merlot serving as great examples.

 The left bank is known for its signature powerhouse Cabs headlined by the likes of Chateau Lafite-Rothschild, Chateau Latour and Chateau Margaux. The right bank is known for its velvety Merlots headlined by the likes of Chateau Cheval Blanc, Chateau Le Pin and Chateau Petrus. Any of these wines in a good vintage will routinely sell for over $1,000 a bottle!

You can find red Bordeaux at just about any price point between $10 and $10,000. If you enjoyed either your left bank or right bank Bordeaux, try another wine from the same side from a different producer or vintage to see if you're forming a real preference. This could be the start of a budding enthusiasm for this highly respected region.

All For Syrah/Shiraz

Level		Bottles		Price	

Wines to Buy:	This activity features two common and very affordable wines, so expect to pay around $10-$15 for each. The first bottle you'll need is a Côtes du Rhône (Coat do ROW-n) from Southern France. Check the blend on the label or ask your wine store to make sure it's a "GSM blend", meaning it is comprised of Grenache, Syrah and Mouvèdre grapes. Nearly all wines labeled Côtes du Rhône or Châteauneuf-du-Pape, a sub-region of the Rhône Valley, will be a GSM blend. The second bottle you'll need is a 100% Shiraz [Shir-RAWZ] from Australia. You've likely seen some of the popular brands in this space including Yellow Tail, Layer Cake and Hardys, and any of them will do just fine.
What to Expect:	We'll be comparing a classic "GSM blend" from the Rhône Valley, one of the premiere wine-growing regions in the world, with an Australian Shiraz. Syrah [Sir-AH], or Shiraz as the Australians call it, is one of the key component grapes in a GSM blend and provides the wine with some of its most distinguishing characteristics. This activity will show not only the difference in regional styles, but also the characteristics of Syrah that make it such an important part of the GSM blend. Note that the Côtes du Rhône is typically mostly Grenache, with a small amount of Syrah, while the Australian Shiraz will consist 100% of Syrah grapes.

 What's the difference between Syrah and Shiraz? Genetically speaking, nothing. They are the same grape. But given consumers' association of Shiraz with the Australian expression of the grape, many producers world-wide are labelling their bottles Shiraz to signal a more new world style wine and Syrah to signal a more old world style wine. To make matters more confusing, you may wonder how Petite Sirah [Pet-EE sir-AH] fits in the picture. That is a related, but different grape variety all together!

Pop those corks and pour a glass of each bottle! You should immediately notice a stark difference in color. The Australian Shiraz should appear purple and almost inky; whereas the GSM should be quite a bit lighter. This is because Grenache generally produces a very light wine, while Syrah / Shiraz is one of the darkest wines you can find. Syrah / Shiraz grapes are small with thick, dark skins and produce wines that are medium to high in acidity and high in tannins. Syrah is often used as a blending grape to provide the backbone, tannic structure and color to a wine (as with the GSM blend), but is also commonly found on its own. Given its structure, Syrah can stand up to long periods of aging with some connoisseurs demanding that a proper Syrah be aged no less than five years (and often 25+ years)!

These are also perfect wines for the **Old World vs. New World** activity earlier in the book.

GSM Blend

To explore the GSM blend, let's first focus on the "G" or Grenache. If you were having a bottle of 100% Grenache, you may find it similar to Pinot Noir as they both tend to be light to medium-bodied wines with a similar aroma and flavor profile. But Grenache is typically higher in alcohol content and lower in acidity. Grenache can age very well, taking on leather and toffee notes over time. If you are drinking a Côtes du Rhône, more likely it's a bit younger and you would find red fruits notes such as strawberry and raspberry.

 Grenache is also widely grown in the Rioja and Priorat regions of Spain where it is called Garnacha. The Priorat style is remarkably different that most other Grenache as the region's unique combination of old vines and steeply terraced land produces powerful wines that are richly concentrated with full tannins, closer to a Cabernet Sauvignon than a Pinot Noir! For ambitious readers, you could do a Rhône Valley Grenache vs. a Priorat vs. an Australian Grenache tasting! Aged Grenache from major Australian producers such as Clarendon Hills and Penfolds can be found in the $30 range and is worth the occasional splurge!

Take a deep whiff of the GSM blend. What do you get on the nose? Do you find hints of red fruits coming from the Grenache? Are there black fruit (blackberry) or black pepper aromas, which are the hallmark of moderate climate Syrah? Don't worry if you don't smell black pepper – in fact it is the most single most common aroma blind spot – as much as 20% of the population simply cannot smell black pepper!

Now let's take a sip. Do you taste what you smell? What flavors hit you first and which flavors linger?

Like the nose characteristics, Syrah typically brings a dark fruit flavor profile with herbaceous or savory and meaty notes that dissipate to a peppery finish. Syrah and Grenache form a similar pair as Cabernet Sauvignon and Merlot, where the Syrah provides the color, tannin, acidity and dark fruit character while Grenache provides the higher alcohol content, lowers the acidity and adds softer red fruit character. The addition of Mouvèdre can bring spice and dark chocolate notes to the blend.

Australian Shiraz

Moving on to the Australian Shiraz, as we mentioned previously, you should notice this wine is a lot darker than the GSM blend. Without the lighter qualities of the Grenache, you should find this wine to be much fuller-bodied. Australian Shiraz has the reputation of being a high-alcohol, fruit bomb, and sometimes the bad reputation of tasting a bit like cough syrup. However, there's plenty of Australian Shiraz that brings all the power and ripe fruit of the grape without the punch in the face.

As you smell the wine, do you notice any of the same black fruit and pepper characteristics to the GSM blend? Most Australian Shiraz also spend time aging in oak, so you may also get vanilla, coconut and toast aromas from the wood contact.

Take a sip. Are you immediately hit by the intense fruit flavors such as blackberries and plums?
Do you find chocolate or licorice notes?
Can you perceive a higher alcohol content?
The warmer Australian climate lends itself to producing wines that have more intense, jammy fruit flavors and higher alcohol. However, Australia is a big country. In cooler regions like the Yarra Valley or Coonawarra (northern Australian regions), you may find more red fruit and pepper notes with higher acidity. In the warmest regions, such as Barossa Valley or McLaren Vale, you'll find more of the big, ripe, dark fruit flavors.

Conclusion

In the end, what did you prefer? Do you like the more nuanced flavors of the GSM blend or do you prefer the bold flavors from the Australian Shiraz?

If you liked the Australian Shiraz, you may also like a California variety such as Shiraz from Clos du Bois or Francis Coppola. If you liked the GSM blend, you could try a 100% Syrah from the Hermitage region of Northern Rhône from producers such as M. Chapoutier, Guigal or Jaboulet (although these will be at a higher price point)!

> Another common blend with Syrah is the white wine grape Viognier. This unique blend of red and white grapes is especially popular in the Northern Rhône valley where the introduction of Viognier grapes during fermentation lends a smoother texture and exotic fruit notes to the resulting wine. Check out the **Virtual Tour of the Rhône Valley** activity earlier in this book to dive into more detail.

All For Dessert Wine

Level		Bottles		Price	
Level	*(gauge icon)*	Bottles	*(bottle icons)* or	Price	$$\$\$\$\$$$

Wines to Buy:	Don't try to drink all the wines we discuss in this activity in the same sitting! When it comes to sweet wines a little goes a long way, and your palate will tire of these more quickly than dry wines. Instead of tackling this all at once we'd recommend picking a single wine to start and come back to this activity with different wines over time. A sweet Riesling would be a good way to start. Ask your local wine merchant for a Riesling produced with Süssreserve (SEUSS-reserve). Port is also a good first wine for this activity as it's easy to find and perfectly fine versions can be had for less than $15. Ice wine is becoming more common, especially in colder areas where it may be produced locally, though may be more expensive at $20 or so for a half bottle. Italian Vin Santo is somewhat less common, but a half bottle shouldn't be hard to find for less than $20 at a good wine shop. Sauternes can be outrageously expensive, but ask your local wine merchant if they have an affordable bottle, or perhaps a Barsac [BAHR-sahk], a slightly cheaper alternative from a neighboring region, instead.
What to Expect:	Dessert wines are a funny bunch. Many are relegated to the bargain bin and generally scoffed at as being too cloying and overtly sugary to have any sophisticated appeal. But at their finest they are some of the most highly regarded and age-worthy wines in the world. You've probably heard of Port, and perhaps ice wine or Sauternes, and this activity will give you the opportunity to try these as well as several other sweet wines. We organize the wines based on how they are produced so you get a sense of the effort that goes into producing such a sweet outcome. Enjoy!

There are three main approaches to producing sweet wine. The first is to simply add a sweet component to an existing dry wine. The second is to interrupt the fermentation process that converts sugar to alcohol such that some sugar remains. And finally you can start with sweeter grapes to begin with so that when fermentation completes the yeast has not been able to consume all of the sugar. We'll step though examples of wine produced using each of these methods. Based on the wine you've selected go ahead and skip to that section of this activity.

Add a sweet component to an existing dry wine
Recommended wine: Riesling produced with Süssreserve

Go ahead and pour everyone a glass and start by noticing the viscosity of your wine. Swirl your glass to produce "legs" that fall down the edge. Do the legs last longer than your typical wine? Some Rieslings with a sweet component added to the wine will be slightly more viscous or thicker, hinting at the full, round flavors to follow. Swirl and smell your wine and consider the major aromas you detect. As we've discussed earlier in this book, you cannot smell sugar, but you can smell other characteristics typically associated with sweets such as tropical fruits (think mangos and pineapple) and stone fruits (especially peaches).

Based on the viscosity and aroma of your wine, consider what you expect it to taste like before taking your first sip. Have a drink. Were your expectations met or was this a surprise?
Are you finding tropical and stone fruit flavors, or something else?
Consider next the balance of acidity and sugar. After you've taken a sip, are your salivary glands still active due to the acid, or is there a residual sweetness that remains on your tongue?

This may feel like cheating, but adding a sweet component to an existing dry wine is a perfectly acceptable way to produce a dessert wine. This is in fact the most common method for producing sweet Riesling. At the end of the production process the winemaker will simply add an element of unfermented grape juice called Süssreserve, meaning "sweet reserve", into the wine with the resulting product no more than 15% juice. This grape juice is more viscous than the base wine, which is why you may have noticed the longer legs when swirling your glass. Furthermore, by adding the grape juice, the sugar content increases and the alcohol decreases. This explains why you likely experienced a residual sweetness on your tongue even after swallowing.

For many drinkers, sweet Riesling is their entry into the world of wine because it's so easy to enjoy due to its low alcohol. Interest wanes over time for those who get serious about wine because most sweet Rieslings taste fairly similar: tropical and stone fruit aroma and taste, with some residual sugar. These wines do offer great pairing opportunities though, and would work not only as a dessert but also with spicy dishes, especially Asian cuisine.

This technique of adding juice to the wine is typically reserved for less expensive Kabinett and Spätlese level wines that do not require prolonged aging of the grapes to produce higher sugar levels. See the **All For Riesling** activity earlier in this book to explore this great wine in more detail.

Interrupt the fermentation process
Recommended wine: Tawny or Ruby Port
Given their high sugar levels and intense flavors, these dessert wines are typically enjoyed in small amounts, so pour everyone a small glass, about half the amount of a normal pour. Don't worry, you can always pour another round or three later.

There are two major styles of Port: Ruby and Tawny. Depending on the style you've selected for this activity you will have one of two very different experiences. While it will be clearly labeled on the bottle, you can actually tell which style of Port you have in front of you simply by looking at the wine. Ruby Port, as its name implies, will be a deep red, garnet color. Tawny Port on the other hand, will have a brown, rusty color. These color differences arise due to the wines' production methods. Ruby Port is aged for a few years in concrete or stainless steel barrels that prevent oxidation, and thus retains its dark red color. Tawny Port is aged far longer, even for decades, in wooden barrels that allow some exposure to oxygen. During the aging period the wine will lose its red color as it turns rusty brown.

In another case of sneaky marketing in the wine industry, Port is often advertised with an age statement prominently displayed on the bottle to convince you of the quality of its contents. However, be aware that the age stated on the bottle is an *average* of the wines used in the blend. Not as bad as some spirits that print age statements based purely on the oldest spirit in their blends, but not entirely forthright either.

Based solely on the colors, hazard a guess as to the aromas and flavors you'll find with each of these wines. Which would you expect to have a red fruit character, and which would you expect to be dominated by dried fruits. Which would taste more like caramel? Smell and taste your wine to see if it matches your expectations.

Ruby Port is generally sweeter and dominated by a red fruit character. Tawny Port will lose much of its fruity sweetness as it gains other complexities over the course of aging. It has a hallmark nutty character both on the nose and palate. If it's old enough (20 years or more), it can take on caramel and dried fruit flavors.

In some sense the production of Port is the opposite of the Riesling discussed earlier in this activity. Whereas the Riesling had sweet juice added to the final wine to introduce additional sugars, Port has a high-proof spirit added to an "in-progress" wine to stop the fermenting process before the yeast has dissolved all the sugars. The addition of the spirit, always Brandy in the case of Port, raises the alcohol level of the wine to the point where the yeast responsible for fermentation can no longer survive. The fermentation thus stops before all the sugar has been turned into alcohol and some of the natural sweetness of the grape is preserved in the finished wine. So Riesling has added sugar, but Port has added alcohol to preserve existing sugars. The resulting Port is typically around 80% wine and 20% Brandy. This process of killing the yeast by adding alcohol is called fortification, and Port is just one example of a fortified wine, in this case from the Douro Valley in northern Portugal.

With this in mind, have another taste of your Port and see if you can find that 20% Brandy that's been blended with the wine. It brings added alcohol and heat, so you may feel it in your throat as much as you taste it on your tongue. Quality Port won't produce a harsh burn, but you should notice greater heat than a typical dry red wine since Port is typically around 19% ABV compared to less than 15% for most dry red wines.

 There is in fact a third type of Port called Vintage Port that remains in oak barrels for only two years before bottling, and so retains a deep red color and sweet, ripe fruit flavors while introducing slight elements of wood aging. Vintage Ports are made entirely from a single declared vintage year and known for their extreme aging potential. Given the care that goes into their craftsmanship they are typically significantly more expensive than Ruby or Tawny Ports and intended to age for decades before drinking. If you're looking for a gift that can evolve over a long period of time, perhaps to newlyweds or new parents, Vintage Port would be an ideal choice.

Start with sweeter grapes
Recommended wine: Ice wine, Vin Santo or Sauternes
So far we've talked about two approaches to producing a sweet wine: adding in sweet juice to an already finished wine as is done with some Rieslings, and adding in a high-proof spirit to an "in-progress" wine to stop fermentation and preserve sugars in the underlying wine as is done to produce Port. The third approach to create a sweet wine is to not add anything to the wine, but instead start with grapes with a very high sugar content in the first place. Because the yeast that converts sugar to alcohol dies when the wine reaches 15% ABV, any sugar that remains at that point will be present in the resulting wine. There are three primary ways to source grapes with such a high concentration of sugars, each producing a

different style of wine. Any of these will work for this activity, so go ahead and open whatever you've selected and pour a very small amount, say a quarter of a usual glass, and get to smelling and tasting.

Eiswein / ice wine

If you've selected an Eiswein for this activity it's likely from a cold region such as Canada or Germany. Can you figure out why grapes from cold regions are used to produce sweet wines? Hint: look no further than the very term "ice wine." These wines are produced from grapes that have literally frozen on the vine. Freezing fruits greatly enhances their sweet flavors by removing much of the water trapped within. As an experiment to prove this out, next time you have a basket of strawberries place one in the freezer overnight and thaw it out the next day. The resulting strawberry will be noticeably smaller than before, and now intensely sweet. Ice wines follow the exact same principle. Its take more grapes to produce the wine, but the result is rich and intensely flavored. The sheer quantity of grapes required to produce these wines is a main driver for their high price.

What aromas and flavors are you getting? How would you describe the overall body and structure of your wine? Ice wines are generally described as luscious, rich, syrupy and intense. You may find flavors of peach, apricot, mango and honey. They are not light on the palate in the same way that Riesling or Port can be and therefore are best in small quantities.

Can you think of pairing opportunities for such a powerful wine? You'd need food that matches the rich, sweet character of the wine, so a dense fruit cake or pudding could work well.

Vin Santo

Another way to start with sweet grapes is to dry them before the winemaking process, essentially making wine from raisins! Vin Santo is an Italian dessert wine produced from grapes that have been dried out on straw mats for several months. The raisins are then pressed and fermentation takes place in wooden barrels. Like ice wine, Vin Santo is relatively expensive due to this labor intensive process. What do you think of the wine?

Notice how its high viscosity causes it to stick to the sides of your glass as you swirl. What aromas and flavors do you experience? Vin Santo is typically deeper and darker in character than ice wine with primary flavors of dried stone fruits, nuts, honey and caramel.

Can you pick out flavors originating from the grapes versus those originating from the wood treatment in the barrel? Biscotti is the classic food pairing with Vin Santo where the dry, nutty character of the food fits well with the dried fruit character of the wine.

Sauternes

The third and final technique we'll describe for obtaining sweet grapes is perhaps the most surprising: picking rotten grapes. The famed Sauternes and Barsac dessert wines of Bordeaux are produced from grapes affected by what the French, in their marketing genius, dub "noble rot." Due to their location nestled amidst rivers and hills, and the predominantly cool evening weather, the Sauternes and Barsac regions of Bordeaux are uniquely situated in an area that is susceptible to heavy fog in the early morning hours. As the sun rises the fog settles, leaving a dewy mist on the grapes. The sun in turn warms the moisture on the grapes which leads to the fruit gently rotting in the hot midday heat. Late in the growing seasons when the grapes have fully ripened, under the right foggy conditions, grapes will be hand-picked from the vines every morning for optimal selection: just enough rot that the grapes have started to shrivel and condense their sugars, but not so much that they've simply gone bad. This process is hugely labor intensive in even the best years. In the worst years when the climate doesn't cooperate, the rot does not form and the wines are not produced.

Go ahead and pour a small glass for everyone and enjoy. What aromas and flavors do you detect? Sauternes and Barsac are renowned for their character of golden raisins, bruised golden apple, grapefruit, tropical fruits and lemon zest.

What do you think of the aging potential of this wine? Best enjoyed young, or let to sit for a few years? Sauternes in particular is known for its extreme ability to age, gaining depth and complexity for decades. What may start out as a bright yellow, citrus-dominated, lip-puckering wine, may, after a few decades under proper conditions, evolve into an amber-hued, nutty, caramel and dried stone-fruit masterpiece. Château d'Yquem produces the most renowned Sauternes in the world, with new bottles selling for hundreds of dollars, and vintage bottles selling for thousands.

Though these are sweet wines, the classic pairing with Sauternes and Barsac is foie gras where the sweet, syrupy wine balances out the rich, unctuous foie.

> The dessert wines of Sauternes and Barsac are made from the same grapes as Bordeaux's dry white wines: Sauvignon Blanc and Semillion. Check out the **All For Sauvignon Blanc and Pinot Gris/Grigio** activity earlier in this book to experience a very different expression of the same underlying grape.

Conclusion

A wine's individual components are not experienced in isolation, but rather in relation to each other. When considering taste and looking for key components of sweetness and acid, remember that the sugars in a sweeter wine will mask some of the acidity. For this reason dessert wines can taste very low in acid at first. But try to analyze each component of a wine on both the attack, mid-palate and finish. A wine that tastes low acid on the attack (such as most dessert wines) will often express its acidity on the mid-palate and finish. What initially tastes low in acidity may finish as a medium acid wine. All well-made dessert wines, even the very sweetest examples, will remain balanced and enjoyable. Perhaps more than any other wines, particular care should be paid to pairing dessert wines with food since their extreme sweetness requires food substantial enough to contribute to a balanced experience.

Wine Journal

About the Wine	About the Tasting
Producer	Date
Name	Location
Region	People
Vintage	Food pairing
Grape(s)	Decanted?
Alcohol %	Temperature
References/Notes	Purchase price/location/date

Upon Opening

Appearance

Aroma

Taste

After __ minutes/hours

Appearance

Aroma

Taste

After __ minutes/hours

Appearance

Aroma

Taste

Conclusion

Rating
1 - Faulty
2 - Poor
3 - Average
4 - Good
5 - Outstanding

Recommended Pairing

Pronunciation Guide

Asti [AH-stee]
Auslese [AUS-lessa]
Barbaresco [Bar-bar-ES-co]
Barbera [Bar-BEAR-ah]
Barolo [Bar-OH-low]
Barsac [BAHR-sahk]
Beaujolais [BO-JA-lay]
Bordeaux [Boar-DOUGH]
Cabernet Sauvignon [Cab-er-NAY so-vin-yown]
Cahors [Kay-HOR]
Carménère [Car-men-YAIR]
Cava [KAH-va]
Chablis [Sha-BLEE]
Champagne [SHAM-pain]
Chardonnay [Shar-done-AY]
Charmat [Shar MAH]
Châteauneuf-du-Pape [Shat-en-OOF du POP]
Chianti [Kee-YAWN-tee]
Côte-Rôties [Coat ro-TEE]
Côtes du Rhône [Coat do ROW-n]
Crémant [cray-MAWN]
Crozes-Hermitage [Crow-ZAY er-mi-TAHJ]
Dolcetto [Dul-CHET-oh]
Fumé Blanc [Foo-MAY blawnk]
Gamay [Gam-MAY]
Garnacha [Gar-NACH-ah]
Gewürztraminer [Guh-VERTZ-tra-meen-er]
Gigondes [Jhee-gone-DAS]
Grenache [Gren-AWSH]
Langhe [LANG-eh]
Mâconnais [MAK-oh-nay]
Malbec [MAL-bek]

Melon de Bourgogne [Mel-OWN duh boar-GOAN]
Merlot [Mer-LOW]
Montepulciano [MON-teh-PULL-che-AH-no]
Mouvèdre [Moo-VEH-drah]
Muscadelle [Moos-kah-DELL]
Muscadet [Moos-kah-DAY]
Muscat [Moos-KAHT]
Nebbiolos [Neb-ee-OH-lo]
Petit Verdot [Pe-TEE ver-DOUGH]
Piedmont [PEED-mont]
Pinot Grigio [PEE-no GREE-jee-oh]
Pinot Gris [PEE-no GREE]
Pinot Meunier [PEE-no min-ur]
Pinot Noir [PEE-no nwar]
Priorat [PROY-rot]
Prosecco [Pro-SEK-oh]
Riesling [REE-sling]
Rioja [Ree-OH-ha]
Sangiovese [San-JOE-vase-eh]
Sauternes [Saw-TURN]
Sauvignon Blanc [SO-vin-yown BLAWNK]
Sémillon [Sem-ee-OWN]
Shiraz [Shir-RAWZ]
Spätlese [SPET-less-a]
Spumante [Spoo-MAWN-tay]
Syrah [Sir-AH]
Tempranillo [Temp-ra-NEE-yo]
Vinsobres [Vin-SOBE]
Viognier [Vee-yo-NAY]
Willamette [Will-AM-it]
Zinfandel [ZIN-fan-del]

Index: Activities by Number of Bottles

Made in the USA
Middletown, DE
30 March 2019